THE WORLD'S BEST
SWIMMING POOLS

Stefanie Waldek

Table of contents

AFRICA

Botswana
WILDERNESS DUMATAU CAMP	10
WILDERNESS JAO CAMP	12
WILDERNESS MOMBO CAMP	14

Kenya
ANDBEYOND KICHWA TEMBO TENTED CAMP	18
OL MALO	20

Mauritius
THE OBEROI BEACH RESORT MAURITIUS	22

Morocco
LA MAMOUNIA	24
KASBAH BELDI	26

Namibia
ANDBEYOND SOSSUSVLEI DESERT LODGE	28
CHIWANI SAFARI CAMPS – MOWANI MOUNTAIN CAMP	30
CHIWANI SAFARI CAMPS – CAMP KIPWE	32
ZANNIER HOTELS OMAANDA	34
WILDERNESS HOANIB SKELETON COAST CAMP	36
ZANNIER HOTELS SONOP	38

Sao Tomé and Principe
SUNDY PRAIA	40

Seychelles
SIX SENSES ZIL PASYON	42

South Africa
THE SILO HOTEL	44
THE SAXON HOTEL, VILLAS & SPA	46
ANDBEYOND TENGILE RIVER LODGE	48
MORUKURU OWNER'S HOUSE	50
DALEBROOK TIDAL POOL	52
ANDBEYOND PHINDA ROCK LODGE	54
ANDBEYOND PHINDA HOMESTEAD	56
ANDBEYOND NGALA SAFARI LODGE	58

Tanzania
ANDBEYOND GRUMETI SERENGETI RIVER LODGE	60
SINGITA SASAKWA LODGE	62
ELEWANA KILINDI ZANZIBAR	64
MWIBA LODGE	66
LEMALA MPINGO RIDGE LODGE	70

Uganda
LEMALA WILDWATERS LODGE	72

Zambia
TONGABEZI LODGE	74
CHIKUNTO SAFARI LODGE	76

Zimbabwe
AMALINDA LODGE	78
SINGITA PAMUSHANA LODGE	80
WILDERNESS LINKWASHA CAMP	82

ASIA & THE MIDDLE EAST

Bhutan
SIX SENSES BHUTAN	84
ANDBEYOND PUNAKHA RIVER LODGE	86

Cambodia
ZANNIER HOTELS PHUM BAITANG	88

India
ANANDA IN THE HIMALAYAS	90
THE OBEROI UDAIVILAS	92
TAJ LAKE PALACE	94
WILDFLOWER HALL, AN OBEROI RESORT	96
SIX SENSES VANA	98

Indonesia
COMO SHAMBHALA ESTATE	100
CAPELLA UBUD	104
THE SANCHAYA	106

Israel
NATURAL POOLS AT GAN HASHLOSHA NATIONAL PARK	108

Japan
HOSHI ONSEN CHOJUKAN	110

Maldives
FAIRMONT MALDIVES, SIRRU FEN FUSHI	112

Nepal
TIGER MOUNTAIN POKHARA LODGE	114

Oman
ANANTARA AL JABAL AL AKHDAR RESORT	116
THE CHEDI MUSCAT	118
BIMMAH SINKHOLE	120

The Philippines
MAGPUPUNGKO ROCK POOLS	122

Singapore
MARINA BAY SANDS	124

Thailand
THE LIBRARY	126
KEEMALA	128
137 PILLARS SUITES & RESIDENCES BANGKOK	130
FOUR SEASONS TENTED CAMP GOLDEN TRIANGLE	132
SIX SENSES YAO NOI	134
FOUR SEASONS RESORT CHIANG MAI	136
FOUR SEASONS RESORT KOH SAMUI	138

Tibet (China)
ST. REGIS LHASA RESORT	140

Türkiye
TITANIC MARDAN PALACE	142
TITANIC GOLF DELUXE BELEK	144
PAMUKKALE TRAVERTINES	146

United Arab Emirates
PARK HYATT DUBAI	148
BURJ AL ARAB JUMEIRAH	150

Vietnam
TOPAS ECOLODGE	154
HÔTEL DES ARTS SAIGON	156
JW MARRIOTT PHU QUOC EMERALD BAY	158
FOUR SEASONS RESORT THE NAM HAI, HOI AN	160
TAI WELLNESS RESORT	162
ZANNIER HOTELS BAI SAN HÔ	164

EUROPE

Austria
AMALIENBAD	166

Croatia
SUN GARDENS DUBROVNIK	168

Denmark
MANON LES SUITES	170

France
ROYAL CHAMPAGNE HOTEL & SPA	172
HÔTEL CRILLON LE BRAVE	174
HÔTEL LES ROCHES ROUGES	178
SHANGRI-LA PARIS	180
PISCINES NATURELLES DE CAVU	182
LA PISCINE DE BON-SECOURS	184

Germany
TROPICAL ISLANDS RESORT	186

Greece
CALILO	188
ASTARTE SUITES	190
KATIKIES CHROMATA	192
CANAVES OIA SUITES, A CANAVES COLLECTION HOTEL	196
GIOLA LAGOON	198
ANDRONIS ARCADIA	200
CANAVES EPITOME, A CANAVES COLLECTION RESORT	202
CRETAN MALIA PARK	204

Hungary
GELLERT THERMAL BATH	208
SZECHENYI BATHS	210

Iceland
ION ADVENTURE HOTEL	212
ELEVEN DEPLAR FARM	214
SELJAVALLALAUG	218

Ireland
    ASHFORD CASTLE — 220

Italy
    GRAND HOTEL TREMEZZO — 222
    ALPIN PANORAMA HOTEL HUBERTUS — 224
    IL SERENO — 226
    MONASTERO SANTA ROSA HOTEL & SPA — 228
    ROCCA DELLE TRE CONTRADE — 230
    GROTTA DELLA POESIA — 232
    HOTEL CIPRIANI, A BELMOND HOTEL — 234
    LE CASCATE DEL MULINO — 238
    MANDARIN ORIENTAL, LAGO DI COMO — 240

Poland
    ZAKRZOWEK PARK POOLS — 242

Portugal
    ALBATROZ BEACH & YACHT CLUB — 244
    DA LINCENCA — 246
    VENTOZELO HOTEL & QUINTA — 248
    PENHA LONGA RESORT — 250
    CAMPO DE ARROZ — 252
    PORTO MONIZ NATURAL SWIMMING POOLS — 254
    TIDAL POOLS OF LECA DA PALMEIRA — 256

Spain
    MANDARIN ORIENTAL, BARCELONA — 258
    CAP ROCAT — 260
    CHARCO DE LA LAJA — 262
    LAS SALINAS DE AGAETE — 264

Switzerland
    HOTEL VILLA HONEGG — 266
    BÜRGENSTOCK RESORT LAKE LUCERNE — 268
    7132 THERMAL BATHS — 270

United Kingdom
    TUNNELS BEACH — 272
    JUBILEE POOL — 274
    TINSIDE LIDO — 276
    EMBASSY GARDENS SKY POOL — 278
    SHOALSTONE POOL — 282
    FAIRY POOLS — 284

NORTH & MIDDLE AMERICA

Anguilla
    CAP JULUCA, A BELMOND HOTEL — 286

Aruba
    CONCHI NATURAL POOL — 290

British Virgin Islands
    THE BATHS — 292

Costa Rica
- PACUARE LODGE — 294
- NAYARA TENTED CAMP — 296
- VILLA AVELLANA — 298

Greenland
- UUNARTOQ HOT SPRING — 300

Grenada
- SILVERSANDS GRENADA — 302

Mexico
- WALDORF ASTORIA LOS CABOS PEDREGAL — 304
- CAREYES — 308
- LAS VENTANAS AL PARAISO, A ROSEWOOD RESORT — 310
- PUNTA CALIZA — 312
- CASA O'TE MITI — 316
- CASA INSPIRACION — 318
- CENOTE XCANAHALTUN — 320
- HIERVE EL AGUA — 322
- ACRE RESORT CABO — 324

Puerto Rico
- DORADO BEACH, A RITZ-CARLTON RESERVE — 326

Saint Kitts and Nevis
- BELLE MONT FARM — 328

St. Lucia
- JADE MOUNTAIN RESORT — 330

Saint Vincent and the Grenadines
- MANDARIN ORIENTAL, CANOUAN — 332

Turks and Caicos
- WYMARA TURKS AND CAICOS — 334

United States
- SHERATON WAIKIKI — 338
- THE SAGAMORE RESORT — 340
- GINNIE SPRINGS — 342
- LOWER FALLS AT ROBERT H. TREMAN STATE PARK — 344
- GARDEN OF THE GODS RESORT & CLUB — 346
- POST RANCH INN — 348
- ENCHANTMENT RESORT — 350
- HAVASU FALLS — 352
- BEVERLY HILLS HOTEL — 354
- BARTON SPRINGS POOL — 356
- FOUR SEASONS HUALALAI — 358
- TRAVERTINE HOT SPRINGS — 360
- TWA HOTEL — 362
- CASTLE HOT SPRINGS — 364
- HAMILTON POOL PRESERVE — 366
- MIRADA LAGOON — 368
- THREE SISTER SPRINGS — 370
- HOTEL FIGUEROA — 372
- VIKING OCTANTIS AND VIKING POLARIS — 374

OCEANIA

Australia
MONA VALE ROCKPOOL	376
BRONTE BATHS	378
DAWN FRASER BATHS	380
ROSS JONES MEMORIAL POOL	382
CARDWELL SPA POOL	384
BOGEY HOLE	386

French Polynesia
NUKUTEPIPI PRIVATE ISLAND	388
FOUR SEASONS RESORT BORA BORA	390
ST. REGIS BORA BORA	394

New Caledonia
PISCINE NATURELLE D'ORO	396

New Zealand
HUKA LODGE	398
ST. CLAIR HOT SALT WATER POOL	400
ARO HA WELLNESS RETREAT	402

Samoa
TO-SUA OCEAN TRENCH	404

Vanuatu
NANDA BLUE HOLE	406

SOUTH AMERICA

Argentina
ENTRE CIELOS WINE & WELLNESS HOTEL	408
FOUR SEASONS BUENOS AIRES	410

Brazil
LAGOONS AT LENCOIS MARANHENSES NATIONAL PARK	412
JW MARRIOTT HOTEL SÃO PAULO	414
HOTEL FASANO RIO DE JANEIRO	416

Chile
SAN ALFONSO DEL MAR	418
VIK CHILE	420
TIERRA PATAGONIA HOTEL & SPA	424
TIERRA ATACAMA HOTEL & SPA	426
WARA HOTEL	428
TIERRA CHILOE	430
LAGUNA CEJAR	432

Colombia
CASA SAN AGUSTIN	434

Ecuador
PIKAIA LODGE	438
FINCH BAY GALAPAGOS HOTEL	440
LAS GRIETAS	442

AFRICA

WILDERNESS DUMATAU CAMP | Linyanti Wildlife Reserve | BOTSWANA

THE WORLD'S BEST SWIMMING POOLS

Located in Botswana's Linyanti Concession, Wilderness DumaTau and its sister camp, Little DumaTau, are tented safari camps set on the waterfront of scenic Osprey Lagoon. Between the two, you'll find an L-shaped pool: one side designed for swimming, another with submerged loungers for sunbathing. Keep your eyes on the lagoon while you're luxuriating here—elephants frequently wade through the reeds. Within the pool complex are shaded day beds, a fitness center, and a deli and bar serving light bites, fresh-pressed juices, and cocktails to keep you energized throughout the day. If you don't feel like taking a dip in the shared pool, each accommodation—a luxe tented suite—has a private plunge pool.

wildernessdestinations.com/africa/botswana/linyanti-region/dumatau-camp

AFRICA

Wilderness Jao is a triumph of safari architecture, successfully creating something unlike the hundreds of lodges found across the continent. Its main hub is a dramatic tree house with glass walls and a thatched roof made of recycled plastic, and a wood boardwalk connects it to the sprawling villas. The pool, too, is an architectural stunner—it's ensconced in a bird's nest–like structure, set on the waters of the Okavango Delta. From here, guests can take game drives, view wildlife by boat, or spend time in the on-site double-story library, complete with a giraffe skeleton.

| | **WILDERNESS JAO CAMP** | Moremi Game Reserve, Okavango Delta | **BOTSWANA** |

THE WORLD'S BEST SWIMMING POOLS

wildernessdestinations.com/africa/botswana/okavango-delta/jao-camp

AFRICA

WILDERNESS MOMBO CAMP | Mombo Concession, Moremi Game Reserve, Okavango Delta | BOTSWANA

THE WORLD'S BEST SWIMMING POOLS

Located inside the Moremi Game Reserve—the "place of plenty"—in the Okavango Delta, Wilderness Mombo Camp is the flagship property of luxury travel operator Wilderness, which has a strong presence in southern Africa. And the area is indeed filled with plenty of wildlife. From the community infinity pool and private plunge pools of the nine tented suites, you might see giraffes, zebras, or elephants wandering by—or perhaps even taking a sip from the pools themselves. Mombo's sister property, Wilderness Little Mombo, is just down the road, and it, too, frequently has wildlife interacting with its pools.

wildernessdestinations.com/africa/botswana/okavango-delta/mombo-camp

AFRICA

| | ANDBEYOND KICHWA TEMBO TENTED CAMP | Maasai Mara National Reserve | KENYA |

THE WORLD'S BEST SWIMMING POOLS

A terraced pool overlooks Kenya's iconic Maasai Mara National Reserve at andBeyond Kichwa Tembo Tented Camp, giving it front-row views of the diverse wildlife found here. The safari lodge itself, however, is set on a private concession adjacent to the reserve, along the Saparingo River and below the Oloololo Escarpment. This location couldn't be more ideal for viewing the Great Migration, when more than 1.5 million wildebeest pass through the Mara. Of course, that's not the only wildlife you'll spot here. Kichwa Tembo means "head of the elephant" in Swahili, so there's always a chance you'll see a herd of the giant animals passing by.

andbeyond.com/destinations/africa/kenya/masai-mara-national-park

AFRICA

OL MALO Laikipia KENYA

THE WORLD'S BEST SWIMMING POOLS

Ol Malo is the name of not only the safari camp, but also the 5,000-acre family-run working ranch upon which it sits. (It also means "place of the greater kudu," an antelope found here.) It's located in the northern reaches of Kenya's Laikipia Plateau, where landscapes differ greatly from the Maasai Mara but are no less full of wildlife. The infinity pool takes a natural shape that mimics a watering hole, and thanks to the camp's location on an escarpment, it offers vistas over a vast landscape of wooded hills and valleys.

olmalo.com

AFRICA

| | THE OBEROI BEACH RESORT MAURITIUS | Baie Aux Tortues, Balaclava, Terre Rouge, 20108 | MAURITIUS |

THE WORLD'S BEST SWIMMING POOLS

The Oberoi Beach Resort is an Eden in Mauritius, set within 20 acres of lush gardens on Turtle Bay. There are sandy beaches for those looking to swim in the sea, but you're here for the pools, right? The resort has an adults-only infinity pool with an adjacent bar for all-day-long lounging and dipping, while an adjacent children's pool lets the little ones get in on the fun. For something a little more private, book one of the many pool villas, which range from the 3,500-square-foot luxury villas to the 8,500-square-foot three-bedroom royal villa—both numbers include indoor and outdoor space.

AFRICA

Morocco's grand dame, La Mamounia is the place to stay in Marrakech: the 206-room property first opened its doors in 1923, welcoming A-list guests both then and now. I'd argue every piece of the hotel is photogenic, but it's the subterranean pool in the spa that takes one's breath away. Best of all, you don't need to be a guest to use it. Book a spa treatment, and you'll gain access to the stunning space. The practically palatial outdoor pool holds its own, too, fringed with palms, day beds, and an elegant poolside bar and restaurant.

LA MAMOUNIA	Avenue Bab Jdid, Marrakech, 40040	MOROCCO

AFRICA

About an hour outside of bustling Marrakech, Kasbah Beldi provides a quiet retreat near Lalla Takerkoust Lake in the foothills of the Atlas Mountains, whose snow-capped peaks are visible from across the 37-acre property. Formerly an olive farm, the hotel is now a getaway for city dwellers who come to relax at the two infinity pools, dine at its restaurant, and say hello to the resident sheep. While you're here, don't miss a visit to the hammam to complete a water-focused itinerary. If you're pressed for time on your Moroccan adventure, you can book a day pass to enjoy the pools and the restaurant for a few hours.

| **KASBAH BELDI** | Lac de Lalla Takerkoust, Village de Talet, 42103 | MOROCCO |

THE WORLD'S BEST SWIMMING POOLS

AFRICA

| **ANDBEYOND SOSSUSVLEI DESERT LODGE** | andBeyond Sossusvlei Private Desert Reserve, Namib Desert | NAMIBIA |

THE WORLD'S BEST SWIMMING POOLS

The azure waters of the main infinity pool at andBeyond Sossusvlei Desert Lodge in Namibia starkly contrast the orange-tinged rocks of the surrounding Namib Desert landscape. At this sleekly modern property, it's all about remoteness, which is all the better for adventure activities like quad biking on dusty trails across hills and valleys. (Did I mention the property is set on its own 31,419-acre reserve adjacent to the NamibRand Nature Reserve?) But there's a more laid-back activity waiting for you in the 11 stone- and-glass solar-powered suites, each outfitted with its own private plunge pool: stargazing. If you have questions about the night sky, head for the lodge's on-site observatory, where an expert will guide your stargazing session.

andbeyond.com/destinations/africa/namibia/sossusvlei-desert

AFRICA

| | CHIWANI SAFARI CAMPS – MOWANI MOUNTAIN CAMP | Uibasen-Twyfelfontein Community Conservancy, Damaraland | NAMIBIA |

THE WORLD'S BEST SWIMMING POOLS

From afar, you might not even notice the lodge built into the ochre boulders on a hillside in Namibia's Damaraland desert. That is, of course, by design. The structures at Chiwani Safari Camps' Mowani Mountain Camp have thatched domed roofs that mimic the boulders' rounded forms, and they're built with natural materials that suit the landscape. There's a swimming hole nestled right into the rocks, while some accommodations have their own infinity plunge pools. While you're here, be sure to visit Twyfelfontein, a nearby UNESCO World Heritage Site known for its rock engravings and paintings that date to the Late Stone Age.

AFRICA

| **CHIWANI SAFARI CAMPS – CAMP KIPWE** | Uibasen-Twyfelfontein Community Conservancy, Damaraland | NAMIBIA |

THE WORLD'S BEST SWIMMING POOLS

At eco lodge Camp Kipwe in Namibia's Damaraland, the pool is a delightfully private swimming hole carved out of the camp's massive boulders. Descend the wooden stairs to the lounging platform, furnished with sun beds and umbrellas, then step across the orange-rock patio to dip into the refreshing pool. It's a small spot, but a lovely one nonetheless. For an even more private experience, book one of the luxury suites, which have private heated pools built into their expansive private decks. These pools aren't tucked into the boulders, but rather built atop them, so they offer beautiful views.

chiwani.com/kipwe

AFRICA

Omaanda might be less than an hour outside of Namibia's capital (and largest) city of Windhoek, but just take a look at the infinity-edge lap pool overlooking the savannah—here, you feel as if you're out in the middle of nowhere. The property spans 22,000 acres, though, so there is something to that sense of remoteness. Ten modern thatched-hut accommodations are built around a central social hub—which is where you'll find the pool—and all the architecture highlights traditional Owambo design. Thanks to Omaanda's partnership with the neighboring N/a'an ku sê Foundation, guests can learn about a variety of local conservation projects, including the rehabilitation of wildlife including rhinos and cheetahs.

	ZANNIER HOTELS OMAANDA	Farm n° 78, Rest of Ondekaremba Farm, Kapps Farm, Windhoek East	NAMIBIA

THE WORLD'S BEST SWIMMING POOLS

zannierhotels.com/omaanda/en

AFRICA

WILDERNESS HOANIB SKELETON COAST CAMP	Hoanib River, Kaokoveld	NAMIBIA

THE WORLD'S BEST SWIMMING POOLS

Deep in Namibia's rugged Kaokoveld, two tributaries of the Hoanib River converge in a valley, and it's at this picturesque spot that you'll find Wilderness Hoanib Skeleton Coast Camp. The eight-tent lodge is surrounded by rugged hills, where you might spot desert-adapted elephants and black rhinos that thrive in this unique environment, as well as lions, giraffes, and cheetahs. This is the desert, which means it's typically very hot by day—thus the pool is a welcome respite from the temperatures. At night, however, it cools down dramatically, so you'll want to layer up to go stargazing.

wildernessdestinations.com/africa/namibia/kunene-region/hoanib-skeleton-coast-camp

AFRICA

It might be strange for humans to call a pile of boulders home in this day and age, but guests at Zannier Hotels Sonop will do just that. This 10-tent safari lodge is built into such a pile of boulders deep in the Hardap Region of the Namib Desert on a 13,800-acre reserve. But you certainly won't find bare-bones accommodations here. The tents are furnished with hundreds of antiques that lend a 1920s feel to the property. Amenities include a cocktail and cigar lounge, a spa, a fitness center, and stables —and a heated infinity pool with an attached pool bar.

| | **ZANNIER HOTELS SONOP** | Sonop Farm, Road D707, Hardap Region | NAMIBIA |

THE WORLD'S BEST SWIMMING POOLS

zannierhotels.com/sonop/en/accommodation

AFRICA

 SUNDY PRAIA | Santo António, Príncipe Island | SÃO TOMÉ AND PRÍNCIPE

THE WORLD'S BEST SWIMMING POOLS

Sundy Praia's intimate infinity pool has an almost residential quality to it, as if it might be found in the backyard of a private beachfront mansion. Considering there are only 15 tented villas here, that notion isn't too far off from the truth. The luxe eco resort on the island of Príncipe is just 20 minutes from the airport, but it feels utterly secluded, thanks to its hiding spot within the rainforest. But don't let those trees fool you—this is a beachfront resort, so you get the best of the lush flora and the sea.

hbdprincipe.com/sundy

AFRICA

There's certainly no shortage of pools at Six Senses Zil Pasyon, a private island resort in the Seychelles where each of the 28 villas has its own pool. And that count doesn't even include the shared pools, or the pools of the extraordinary private residences, which look as though they belong in a Hollywood action flick as the home of an eccentric billionaire. Some of the most impressive ones are built atop or into the granite boulders, where the green Sukabumi tiles that line the pool's interior match the hue of the ocean below.

| **SIX SENSES ZIL PASYON** | Félicité | **SEYCHELLES** |

THE WORLD'S BEST SWIMMING POOLS

sixsenses.com/en/resorts/zil-pasyon

AFRICA

THE SILO HOTEL | Silo Square, Victoria & Alfred Waterfront, Cape Town, 8001 | SOUTH AFRICA

THE WORLD'S BEST SWIMMING POOLS

Yes, Cape Town's Silo Hotel is indeed housed in former grain silos. But there's been a radical transformation here, thanks to British designer Thomas Heatherwick. The hotel, which is situated on the floors above the Zeitz Museum of Contemporary Art Africa, is renowned for its "pillowed" windows that are the stuff of sci-fi dreams. Its crowning jewel, however, is the rooftop pool deck, where swimmers are afforded 360-degree views of the city, from Table Mountain to the harbor. There's also a bar and restaurant up here, which is open to the general public. To take a dip, however, you'll need to be a guest in one of the 28 rooms.

theroyalportfolio.com/the-silo-hotel

AFRICA

THE SAXON HOTEL, VILLAS & SPA

36 Saxon Road, Sandhurst, Johannesburg, 2196

SOUTH AFRICA

THE WORLD'S BEST SWIMMING POOLS

The Saxon Hotel in Johannesburg is perhaps best known for its long-term guest, Nelson Mandela, who penned *Long Walk to Freedom* while he was residing here. At that time, the estate was a private home. Now it's a 53-suite hotel, anchored by its enormous swimming pool out front that draws your eye up to the large dome above the reception atrium. It's not the only pool here, though: the three on-property villas also have small pools, if you'd prefer to swim somewhere a little less conspicuous. The property might be in Joburg—albeit in a residential neighborhood—but it feels delightfully like a country estate, thanks largely to its 10 acres of gardens.

AFRICA

ANDBEYOND TENGILE RIVER LODGE | Sabi Sand Game Reserve | SOUTH AFRICA

THE WORLD'S BEST SWIMMING POOLS

Tengile is the Shangaan word for "tranquil," and that's just what andBeyond Tengile River Lodge is. The nine-suite camp is located right on the Sand River within the Sabi Sand Private Game Reserve, and it's not uncommon to see elephants or buffalo in the flowing waters. Each suite is outfitted with its own sizable pool, though there's also a communal lap pool that's a touch longer for more active swims. Off the private pools on the spacious decks is a sunken living room that's perfect for a post-swim snooze. And did I mention the outdoor showers?

AFRICA

MORUKURU OWNER'S HOUSE | Madikwe Game Reserve | SOUTH AFRICA

THE WORLD'S BEST SWIMMING POOLS

As its name implies, Morukuru Owner's House is indeed an exclusive-use safari lodge, one with two bedrooms, a kitchen, a dining room, a living room, and a library. And, of course, there's a pool. Because the home is surrounded by tamboti trees (also known as Morukuru trees in the Tswana language), you feel as if you're in a tree house, with the pool deck presiding over the Marico River below. If you need more space for your group, you can also book the adjacent Morukuru River Lodge, a three-bedroom villa (and yes, it does come with another pool).

morukuru.com/accommodations/morukuru-owners-house

AFRICA

DALEBROOK TIDAL POOL

Dalebrook Road, opposite Kalk Bay Community Centre, St. James, Cape Town, 7946

SOUTH AFRICA

THE WORLD'S BEST SWIMMING POOLS

If you're brave enough to dip into the refreshing waters of False Bay in Cape Town, do so for sunrise at Dalebrook Tidal Pool—you won't regret the view. The pool is located between St. James and Kalk Bay and is a favorite among locals, but visitors are always welcome to go for a swim, too. While False Bay was once known for its resident great white sharks, the apex predators have moved on to new waters. Now, it's fantastic for whale watching, which you can do while sunning yourself on the large boulders in the tidal pool.

AFRICA

The landscape in the Phinda Private Game Reserve, where you'll find andBeyond Phinda Rock Lodge, is surprisingly lush, thanks to its location near the Indian Ocean, which creates coastal rain. And since there's plenty of water, that means there's plenty of wildlife. See everything from the Big Five to hippos and cheetahs across seven distinct ecosystems. The lodge has six suites built into a cliff face, each with a private plunge pool with a panoramic view. It shares the Phinda Private Game Reserve with several other andBeyond properties, including Phinda Homestead.

| | **ANDBEYOND PHINDA ROCK LODGE** | Phinda Private Game Reserve, KwaZulu-Natal, 3936 | SOUTH AFRICA |

THE WORLD'S BEST SWIMMING POOLS

AFRICA

| | **ANDBEYOND PHINDA HOMESTEAD** | Phinda Private Game Reserve, KwaZulu-Natal, 3960 | SOUTH AFRICA |

THE WORLD'S BEST SWIMMING POOLS

The Phinda Private Game Reserve in South Africa's KwaZulu-Natal province spans 73,800 acres of green landscapes, and given that it's home to the Big Five, 436 species of birds, and numerous other creatures, it's a pretty fine place for a safari. If you're looking for exclusivity on the reserve, which hosts several andBeyond lodges, book Phinda Homestead, a four-bedroom private home with a beautiful infinity pool. Just beyond it is a watering hole, so wildlife frequently visits the site. Since your group will be the only one here, your schedule is your own—you're free to relax by the pool as much as you'd like, or organize game drives or other excursions at your leisure.

andbeyond.com/destinations/africa/south-africa/kwazulu-natal

AFRICA

 | **ANDBEYOND NGALA SAFARI LODGE** | Ngala Private Game Reserve, Timbavati, 1380 | SOUTH AFRICA

THE WORLD'S BEST SWIMMING POOLS

Located on the Ngala Private Game Reserve, andBeyond Ngala Safari Lodge is a charming camp with 20 thatched-roof cottages for guests. One of its standouts is its terraced pool, which has a curved shape and a bright-blue hue that contrasts with the watering hole next door. The second standout feature is the fact that the reserve shares an unfenced border with the iconic Kruger National Park—that means the wildlife is free to roam between the two areas, but humans are not. As such, guests at Ngala have a fair bit of exclusivity on the 36,300-acre reserve, sharing it with just one other andBeyond property.

andbeyond.com/destinations/africa/south-africa/kruger-national-park/ngala-private-game-reserve

AFRICA

Tanzania's Serengeti might be one of the most famous—and most popular—safari destinations in Africa, but andBeyond Grumeti Serengeti River Lodge is tucked away in a remote corner of the national park, allowing you to feel blissfully isolated—from humans, that is. Wildlife is, of course, everywhere, with one of the standouts here being the hippos that take up residence in the river just beyond the lodge's communal pool for part of the year. You might even be able to see them from your suite's private plunge pool. Always keep an eye on the riverbank beyond the hippos, though, as you never know what might come by for a drink.

| | **ANDBEYOND GRUMETI SERENGETI RIVER LODGE** | Grumeti Game Reserve | TANZANIA |

THE WORLD'S BEST SWIMMING POOLS

AFRICA

SINGITA SASAKWA LODGE | Sasakwa Hill, Grumeti Game Reserve | **TANZANIA**

62

THE WORLD'S BEST SWIMMING POOLS

Tanzania's Singita Sasakwa Lodge feels like a private Edwardian manor, one that's been updated with just enough 21st-century amenities. As tempting as it might be to while away the day in the luxury of the stately lodge, you're primarily here for the wildlife. That said, you can mix the best of both worlds at the infinity pool. Because the lodge sits on a hilltop, you have vast views over the savannah—over 350,000 private acres, to be exact, adjacent to Serengeti National Park. Each of the cottages has a private plunge pool, too, while the Hillside Suite has a full infinity pool for private use.

AFRICA

| | **ELEWANA KILINDI ZANZIBAR** | Kendwa, on the northwest coast of Zanzibar | TANZANIA |

THE WORLD'S BEST SWIMMING POOLS

About an hour and a half outside Zanzibar's historic Stone Town, Kilindi Zanzibar is where you go to kick back and relax. There are just 15 white-domed suites spread across 52 acres of gardens at this boutique beachfront resort, permitting just about as much solitude as you desire. But if you're feeling a little social, head for the communal T-shaped infinity pool, which is the perfect place to watch the dhows sail past. Plus, this is where you'll find the bar! Fun fact: the hotel was originally built as a private retreat for ABBA's Benny Andersson.

elewanacollection.com/kilindi-zanzibar/at-a-glance

AFRICA

| | **MWIBA LODGE** | Mwiba Wildlife Reserve, Arusha | TANZANIA |

THE WORLD'S BEST SWIMMING POOLS

Built into a hill of stone boulders, Mwiba Lodge overlooks the Arugusinyai River, which flows through the 130,000-acre Mwiba Wildlife Reserve in the southern Serengeti. Its infinity-edge pool sits atop a massive stone wall that's quite impressive from afar —peep it from a helicopter ride past the property— and it looks out over a lush landscape that's a far cry from the open plains you might associate with the Serengeti. There's also a secret plunge pool tucked around a boulder, and it's well worth seeking out. While you're out on your game drive, keep an eye out for leopards. Mwiba is known for sightings of the elusive cat.

legendaryexpeditions.co.tz/mwiba-lodge

AFRICA

LEMALA MPINGO RIDGE LODGE | Tarangire Road, Tarangire National Park | TANZANIA

THE WORLD'S BEST SWIMMING POOLS

The name of this safari camp tells all. The 15-suite Lemala Mpingo Ridge Lodge is indeed located on a ridge. More specifically, a ridge in Tarangire National Park, a rather under-the-radar safari destination in Tanzania, at least compared with the Serengeti and the Ngorongoro Crater. The T-shaped infinity pool overlooks the vast Tarangire savannah, where you'll go on game drives to see elephants, lions, leopards, and birds—lots of birds—among other creatures. One particular treat at Mpingo Ridge is the night game drives, which show you an entirely different side of the savannah.

lemalacamps.com/stay/mpingo-ridge-lodge

AFRICA

| | **LEMALA WILDWATERS LODGE** | Kalagala Island, River Nile | UGANDA |

THE WORLD'S BEST SWIMMING POOLS

The Nile might be most closely associated with Egypt, but its waters flow through many other countries in Africa, including Uganda. Here, you can even stay in a hotel on an island right in the middle of the river. Lemala Wildwaters Lodge on the forested Kalagala Island is surrounded by rapids—it's accessible only by boat, and one of the most popular activities here is, perhaps unsurprisingly, whitewater rafting. One of the calmer ways to take in the excitement, however, is by lounging in the pool, which is built to feel like it's a part of the river.

lemalacamps.com/stay/wildwaters-lodge

AFRICA

Set on the Zambia bank of the mighty Zambezi River, which cascades over Victoria Falls just downriver, Tongabezi Lodge is a quiet retreat. There are just five river cottages and seven private houses here, some of which have private plunge pools. There's a shared pool, too, alongside which is a bar for refreshments. The lodge offers guests guided safaris in the nearby Mosi-oa-Tunya National Park, boat trips on the Zambezi River, day trips to Livingstone, and visits to Victoria Falls—all included in the rate. And you can tack on add-ons like helicopter flights, whitewater rafting, and a ride on the Royal Livingstone Express train.

| | **TONGABEZI LODGE** | Nakatindi Road, Livingstone | ZAMBIA |

THE WORLD'S BEST SWIMMING POOLS

AFRICA

| **CHIKUNTO SAFARI LODGE** | Along Luangwa River, South Luangwa National Park | ZAMBIA |

THE WORLD'S BEST SWIMMING POOLS

Drive about an hour into Zambia's South Luangwa National Park from the Mfuwe gate, and you'll come across Chikunto Safari Lodge, a five-tent property that accommodates just 12 guests at any given time. The intimate camp is built onto a platform above the sandy bank of the Luangwa River—you'll find a lap pool embedded in it, from which you can observe the wildlife coming to drink from the river. When conditions allow, take a walking safari along the river, and during the emerald season, which runs from November through March, explore the river by boat.

chikunto.com

AFRICA

AMALINDA LODGE | Matobo Hills UNESCO World Heritage Site | ZIMBABWE

Zimbabwe's Matobo Hills are a designated UNESCO World Heritage Site renowned for their massive granite boulders—and the ancient art that decorates them. In those rocks, you'll also find Amalinda Lodge, a nine-room boutique camp that incorporates the landscape right into its bones. (There's also a private villa for those seeking more space.) The seamless combination of nature with man-made continues into the zero-entry infinity-edge pool, which is partially made from a natural granite bowl. When you're not cooling off in the blue waters, you can take excursions to see the 13,000-year-old rock art or go rhino tracking.

amalindacollection.com/lodges/amalinda-lodge

AFRICA

SINGITA PAMUSHANA LODGE | Malilangwe Wildlife Reserve | ZIMBABWE

THE WORLD'S BEST SWIMMING POOLS

Right as you enter Singita Pamushana Lodge in Zimbabwe's Malilangwe Wildlife Reserve, you're greeted by a cliff-top infinity pool above the glittering waters of the Malilangwe Dam. Beyond are rolling green hills as far as the eye can see. It's a pretty spectacular vista, but the pool action doesn't end there. Each of the eight suites, as well as the exclusive-use Singita Malilangwe House next door, has its own infinity pool, too, with equally stunning views. Game drives are multifaceted, incorporating much more than just wildlife—your guide will also take you to ancient rock art sites.

AFRICA

WILDERNESS LINKWASHA CAMP | Hwange National Park | ZIMBABWE

THE WORLD'S BEST SWIMMING POOLS

Wilderness Linkwasha has not one, but two private watering holes: one for humans and one for animals, although the animals sometimes like to blur the lines. It's located on a private concession in Zimbabwe's Hwange National Park, right on the edge of the famous Ngamo Plains. The property is a contemporary safari camp in terms of its decor, rather than a traditional one, though it still has tented accommodations (some things are best left untouched). They are, of course, quite luxe and modern, though—this could be considered the top tier of glamping. For a more "out there" experience, book a night in a Star Bed.

ASIA & THE MIDDLE EAST

Six Senses Bhutan isn't a single lodge, but rather a group of five lodges spread across five valleys—Paro, Thimphu, Punakha, Gangtey, and Bumthang—and your visit should include a night or two in each. While all the properties share an ethos of wellness, sustainability, and Bhutanese culture, each has individual character, from a forest-bathing retreat to a crane-spotting paradise. Three of the lodges have pools: there's a sprawling outdoor pool in Punakha, an earthy indoor pool in Paro, and an indoor pool surrounded by floor-to-ceiling windows in Thimphu. Each one is outstanding in its own right.

	SIX SENSES BHUTAN	Chunimeding, Babesa, Chang Gewog, Thimphu	BHUTAN

ASIA & THE MIDDLE EAST

ANDBEYOND PUNAKHA RIVER LODGE | Punakha, 13001 | BHUTAN

THE WORLD'S BEST SWIMMING POOLS

The andBeyond brand's first property in Asia, andBeyond Punakha River Lodge takes a cue from its African safari brethren—it has six luxurious tented suites, plus a one-bedroom suite and a two-bedroom suite. There's a tranquil communal infinity pool with a Bhutanese-style pavilion, and the two suites each have their own plunge pool that turns into a hot tub in the winter. The lodge is located in the Punakha Valley along the Mo Chu River, surrounded by lush forest, and offers a variety of excursions in the region, from rafting, to hiking, to visits to cultural sites, like the Punakha Dzong and the Sangchhen Dorji Lhuendrup Lhakhang Nunnery.

ASIA & THE MIDDLE EAST

ZANNIER HOTELS PHUM BAITANG Neelka Way, Svay Dangkum, Siem Reap, 17252 CAMBODIA

THE WORLD'S BEST SWIMMING POOLS

Though neighboring UNESCO World Heritage Site Angkor Wat is usually the main attraction for travelers visiting Siem Reap, Zannier Hotels Phum Baitang encourages guests to slow down and stay a while. The resort sits on 20 acres of gardens and rice paddies, offering 45 private villas designed in the style of traditional stilted farmhouses, many with private pools, as well as a spa temple whose architecture recalls Angkor Wat. There's also a massive 50-meter infinity pool and a 100-year-old Khmer farmhouse that's now the cocktail hot spot Sunset Lounge. It's easy to spend a few nights or even a week relaxing here and leisurely visiting the nearby attractions.

zannierhotels.com/phumbaitang

ASIA & THE MIDDLE EAST

| | **ANANDA IN THE HIMALAYAS** | The Palace Estate, Narendra Nagar Tehri Garhwal, Uttarakhand, 249175 | INDIA |

THE WORLD'S BEST SWIMMING POOLS

Most guests at Ananda in the Himalayas are there for wellness. This is a destination spa in India, after all, and it offers Ayurvedic, yogic, and meditative programs designed for everything from energy harmonizing to emotional healing. Swimming might not be prescribed for your specific program—your stay is tailored to your wants, needs, and desires—but a stay wouldn't be complete without a dip in the pool. As the main pool is a bit more fitness oriented, I'm particularly drawn to the private pools in the one- and two-bedroom villas, which feel as if they're suspended in the trees.

anandaspa.com

ASIA & THE MIDDLE EAST

THE OBEROI UDAIVILAS

Badi-Gorela-Mulla Talai Road, Haridas Ji Ki Magri, Udaipur, Rajasthan, 313001

INDIA

THE WORLD'S BEST SWIMMING POOLS

The Oberoi Udaivilas in Udaipur, India, is effectively a contemporary palace—it's certainly designed to look like one, and guests are treated like royalty. The property even has a faux moat, which in actuality is a semi-private swimming pool accessible only by guests who book specific rooms. Yes, it's worth the splurge, as the 240-foot-long pool has uninterrupted views of Lake Pichola. Or for something more private, you could book a luxury suite with a private pool. Speaking of private, while the resort might be in a bustling city, it feels delightfully remote thanks to more than 30 acres of gardened grounds.

93   oberoihotels.com/hotels-in-udaipur-udaivilas-resort

ASIA & THE MIDDLE EAST

Built in the mid-18th century, Taj Lake Palace is a Rajnagar marble oasis within Udaipur's Lake Pichola. It was originally a summer resort for Mewar Dynasty rulers, but two centuries later, it opened to the public—and starred in the James Bond film *Octopussy*. The architecture of the palace blends Mewari techniques with a touch of Mughal influence to elegant effect, seen clearly in the ornamentation surrounding the serene pool. There are just 83 rooms and suites here, so it'll never feel too crowded. As the Taj Lake Palace is located on an island, you'll have to take a water taxi to and from the property, which is all the more reason to stay put by the pool all day.

| | **TAJ LAKE PALACE** | Pichola, Udaipur, Rajasthan, 313001 | INDIA |

94

THE WORLD'S BEST SWIMMING POOLS

tajhotels.com/en-in/taj/taj-lake-palace-udaipur

ASIA & THE MIDDLE EAST

| | **WILDFLOWER HALL, AN OBEROI RESORT** | Chharabra, Shimla, Himachal Pradesh, 171012 | INDIA |

THE WORLD'S BEST SWIMMING POOLS

The refined Wildflower Hall, the former estate of British Army commander Lord Kitchener, can be found in the foothills of the Indian Himalayas near the city of Shimla. Of course, those foothills are taller than some mountains themselves—this resort, for instance, sits at 8,251 feet in elevation, surrounded by 23 acres of cedar and pine forest. Considering that it snows here during the winter, the swimming pool at Wildflower Hall is an indoor affair, though an adjacent solarium provides mountain views. There's also an infinity whirlpool just outside for those seeking an alfresco dip.

ASIA & THE MIDDLE EAST

| | **SIX SENSES VANA** | Mussoorie Road, Malsi, Dehradun, Uttarakhand, 248001 | INDIA |

THE WORLD'S BEST SWIMMING POOLS

Six Senses Vana in Dehradun, India, is a bona fide wellness retreat, with multiday programs designed to eliminate all manner of ailments, generally reducing stress and replenishing energy through Ayurvedic and Tibetan medicine. Some treatments even extend into the water. Watsu, for instance, is aquatic bodywork where a massage therapist gently moves your body while you're floating in a pool of warm water. When you're not in guided meditation, a yoga class, or an acupuncture session, you can relax by the serene outdoor pool. Interestingly, the wellness retreat is located within city limits, but looking around the tranquil grounds, you might never be able to tell.

sixsenses.com/en/resorts/vana

ASIA & THE MIDDLE EAST

| | **COMO SHAMBHALA ESTATE** | Banjar Begawan, Desa Melinggih Kelod, Payangan, Gianyar, Bali, 80571 | INDONESIA |

Though it's only six miles outside of Ubud's city center, COMO Shambhala Estate is a wellness retreat that feels a million miles away. Built on a forested hillside above the Ayung River, the property has the perfect setting for guests seeking some kind of wellness transformation, whether spiritual, mental, or physical. You might find it in the outdoor vitality pool during a hydrotherapy treatment, or perhaps it'll occur when you're in your residence's pool. A residence, by the way, is a collection of individual suites that share a pool, a lounge, and a dining area, though there are stand-alone villas with private pools, too.

ASIA & THE MIDDLE EAST

	CAPELLA UBUD	Jalan Raya Dalem, Banjar Triwangsa, Desa Keliki, Kecamatan Tegallalang, Ubud, Gianyar, Bali, 80561	**INDONESIA**

104

THE WORLD'S BEST SWIMMING POOLS

If you thought tented accommodations were just for safari, Capella Ubud proves otherwise. There are 23 tented guest suites across the resort—including a two-bedroom suite—each with a private plunge pool. And while those pools are delightful, it's the communal pool that steals the show. It's an above-ground pool, which is something of a rarity at luxury hotels, but that's by design. With its elevated position, the pool's dazzling zigzag pattern on both its exterior and its interior shines brightly. It creates quite the visual sensation, as do the myriad patterns found all around this maximalist property.

ASIA & THE MIDDLE EAST

Just a 50-minute ferry ride from Singapore is the leisure-driven Bintan Island in Indonesia's Riau Archipelago, where many Singaporeans go for a weekend of R & R. Well-heeled travelers might head for The Sanchaya, a beachfront resort with just 29 suites and villas, as well as a private residence called Vanda Villa, which has its own pool. As you emerge from the main building, you're greeted by a sprawling infinity pool with views out to sea. After you've cooled off with a swim, you can grab a bite at the poolside Tasanee Grill, which serves Thai cuisine.

THE SANCHAYA

Lagoi Bay, Jalan Gurindam Duabelas, Plot 5, Sebong Lagoi, Kecamatan Teluk Sebong, Kabupaten Bintan, Kepulauan Riau, 29155

INDONESIA

THE WORLD'S BEST SWIMMING POOLS

thesanchaya.com

ASIA & THE MIDDLE EAST

	NATURAL POOLS AT GAN HASHLOSHA NATIONAL PARK	Gan HaShlosha National Park	**ISRAEL**

108

THE WORLD'S BEST SWIMMING POOLS

There are many reasons to visit Gan HaShlosha National Park in Israel, also known as the Sahne, not least among them the spring-fed natural pools. These oasis-like pools are a constant 82.4 degrees Fahrenheit all year round, and as such are quite popular with swimmers. Elsewhere in the park, you can visit a garden of bells found at settlements across the country, the ruins of a Roman naumachia theater, and the Museum of Regional and Mediterranean Archaeology, which displays artifacts from Ancient Greece, Rome, Persia, and Egypt.

ASIA & THE MIDDLE EAST

| | **HOSHI ONSEN CHOJUKAN** | 650 Nagai, Minakami-machi, Tone-gun, Gunma, 379-1401 | JAPAN |

Hoshi Onsen Chojukan, a riverside ryokan located in Japan's Joshin'etsukogen National Park, has been welcoming visitors to soak in its hot springs for more than 140 years. While the welcoming hospitality and historic architecture are two highlights of this historic property, the warm waters are the star of the show, and there are three ways to enjoy them. The main cypress bathhouse is called Hoshi No Yu, and it offers mixed bathing. Then there are the indoor–outdoor facilities of Tamaki No Yu, and a ladies-only bathhouse, Choju No Yu. No matter which you choose, you're sure to have an utterly relaxing experience.

ASIA & THE MIDDLE EAST

| | **FAIRMONT MALDIVES, SIRRU FEN FUSHI** | Sirru Fen Fushi, Shaviyani Atoll | MALDIVES |

THE WORLD'S BEST SWIMMING POOLS

There are infinity pools, and there are infinity pools. Fairmont Maldives Sirru Fen Fushi has the latter. It's the longest infinity pool in the Maldives, and it truly does look as if it stretches right out to sea. A few dozen yards off the end of the pool is the *Coralarium*, an art installation by Jason deCaires Taylor that doubles as a coral regeneration project—the only one of its kind in the Maldives. If you'd rather take a dip in the ocean than in the pool (whether the infinity pool or your villa's private one), I'd recommend a snorkel along the 5.5-mile-long house reef.

ASIA & THE MIDDLE EAST

It's all about the view from Tiger Mountain Pokhara Lodge's pool. The resort, located about 30 minutes outside of its namesake city in Nepal, sits on a hillside some 1,000 feet above the valley floor, right across from towering Himalayan peaks. From the pool, you can see no fewer than three of the world's 14 "eight-thousanders," which are mountains that rise above 8,000 meters, or approximately 26,250 feet. Since the 18-room lodge opened in 1998—in a ceremony led by legendary mountaineer Sir Edmund Hillary—it's been a champion of regenerative tourism in the region, minimizing impacts on the environment while supporting the local community.

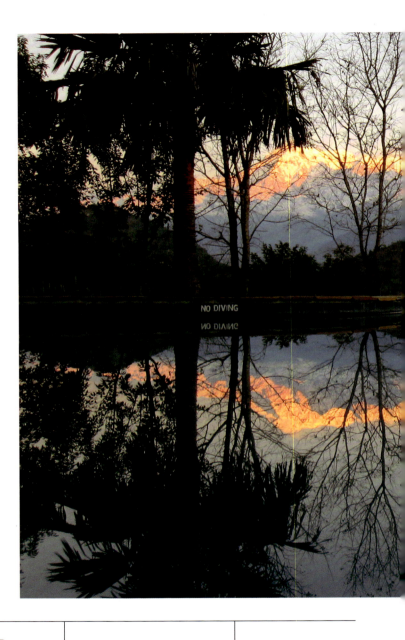

| | **TIGER MOUNTAIN POKHARA LODGE** | Kandani Danda Pokhara 26, Kaski, Gandaki | NEPAL |

THE WORLD'S BEST SWIMMING POOLS

tigermountainpokhara.com

ASIA & THE MIDDLE EAST

| ANANTARA AL JABAL AL AKHDAR RESORT | No. 110, Al Jabal Al Akhdar, Nizwa, 621 | OMAN |

THE WORLD'S BEST SWIMMING POOLS

The communal pool at Anantara Al Jabal Al Akhdar Resort brings you right to a cliff edge on Oman's Jabal Akhdar, or Green Mountain. Needless to say, there's a breathtaking view. There are 82 rooms here with canyon views, but if you're a fan of pools, you'll want to upgrade to one of the 33 villas, each of which has a private pool (and a butler). The hotel is a two-hour drive from Muscat, so between its remoteness and its elevation of 6,500 feet, this place has dark and clear skies perfect for stargazing.

anantara.com/en/jabal-akhdar

ASIA & THE MIDDLE EAST

| | **THE CHEDI MUSCAT** | 18th November Street, Al Khuwair, Muscat | OMAN |

THE WORLD'S BEST SWIMMING POOLS

The Chedi Muscat's palm- and lounger-lined Long Pool is very much appropriately named: it spans an impressive 338 feet, making it the longest in the Middle East. If that weren't enough, there are two other pools here. The Chedi Pool is an infinity-edge stunner fronting the Gulf of Oman, while the shaded Serai Pool is the only spot that welcomes guests of all ages. It's a popular spot for both leisure and business travelers, being about 15 minutes from the airport, three golf courses, the historic Muttrah old town, and Muscat's financial district.

ASIA & THE MIDDLE EAST

 | **BIMMAH SINKHOLE** | Dibab | OMAN

THE WORLD'S BEST SWIMMING POOLS

About a 90-minute drive southeast of Muscat is Hawiyat Najm Park, where you'll find the dazzling Bimmah Sinkhole, known for its turquoise waters that contrast with the orange desert rocks. Though locals traditionally consider the swimming hole a meteorite crater—hawiyat najm loosely translates to "falling star"—it's a naturally occurring sinkhole, where groundwater ate away at the rocks until they collapsed. If you decide to descend the long staircase and take a dip, be aware that modesty is expected of swimmers, so bring appropriate swim apparel. Otherwise, you can also just put your feet in the water and get a pedicure of sorts from the little fish that live there.

ASIA & THE MIDDLE EAST

Surfer's paradise Siargao in the Philippines is an island known for its swell at a spot called Cloud 9. But for those seeking a calmer place to swim, it's all about the Magpupungko Rock Pools. They're located about a 45-minute drive from the Municipality of General Luna and are a popular day trip for swimmers, snorkelers, and cliff jumpers. Keep in mind that these are natural tidal pools, so they exist only during low tide—check your tide charts closely before visiting! If you mistime your visit, you can at least spend your time at the adjacent beach, where you'll find soft sands and a few restaurants.

| **MAGPUPUNGKO ROCK POOLS** | Magpupungko Beach, Siargao Island | **THE PHILIPPINES** |

THE WORLD'S BEST SWIMMING POOLS

ASIA & THE MIDDLE EAST

The rooftop pool at Marina Bay Sands might just be one of the most famous swimming pools in the world. It's truly not hard to see why. For starters, the architecture of the hotel, designed by Moshe Safdie, is particularly striking, with its three towers connected by the sprawling rooftop complex. Then there's the matter of the pool itself—it's the world's largest rooftop infinity pool, sitting pretty on the 57th floor. As such, the views of Singapore's skyline are unparalleled. If you want to visit this iconic pool, there's only one way to do so: book a stay at the hotel.

| | **MARINA BAY SANDS** | 10 Bayfront Avenue, Singapore, 018956 | **SINGAPORE** |

THE WORLD'S BEST SWIMMING POOLS

marinabaysands.com

ASIA & THE MIDDLE EAST

 THE LIBRARY | 14/1 Moo 2, Chaweng Beach, Bophut, Koh Samui, Surat Thani, 84320 | THAILAND

THE WORLD'S BEST SWIMMING POOLS

The Library's pool is one of the more intriguing pools out there. Yes, this beachfront infinity pool is bright red. The design-forward boutique hotel in Koh Samui certainly wasn't afraid to take a chance with the look of its pool, though it's undoubtedly uncanny to go for a swim here. If you'd prefer your pool to be a more traditional color, book a private villa—each one comes with its own green-tiled watering hole. It's worth noting that bold contemporary design is the name of the game at this property, and for that reason, the striking red pool fits in with its surroundings.

ASIA & THE MIDDLE EAST

KEEMALA

10/88 Moo 6, Nakasud Road, Kamala, Kathu, Phuket, 83150

THAILAND

THE WORLD'S BEST SWIMMING POOLS

At Keemala, a hillside resort on Phuket where the jungle meets the beach, the most eye-catching feature might just be the teardrop-shaped Tree Pool Villas tucked into the canopy. Or perhaps it's the woven Bird's Nest Pool Villas. Or maybe… Well, it's probably all of these things. There are four types of villas here, each inspired by the mythical cultures of the region's original inhabitants, and each featuring dramatic architecture—and a pool! But the best pool is the shared one, which has a waterfall and a swim-up bar.

ASIA & THE MIDDLE EAST

While most infinity pools are designed to feel as if they're one with the ocean, the 360-degree rooftop infinity pool at 137 Pillars Suites & Residences Bangkok is designed to feel as if it's one with the sky. That said, if you look down instead of up, you'll see an entirely different view: Bangkok's urban sprawl, which is equally mesmerizing. The rooftop pool isn't the only pool at this hotel—there's a second infinity pool on the 27th floor. Both have adjacent bars and restaurants, but the rooftop eatery is reserved exclusively for hotel guests.

	137 PILLARS SUITES & RESIDENCES BANGKOK	59/1 Sukhumvit Soi 39, Klongton-Nua, Wattana, Bangkok, 10110	THAILAND

THE WORLD'S BEST SWIMMING POOLS

137pillarshotels.com/en/bangkok

ASIA & THE MIDDLE EAST

FOUR SEASONS TENTED CAMP GOLDEN TRIANGLE

499 Moo 1, T. Vieng, Chiang Rai, Chiang Saen District, Chiang Rai, 57150

THAILAND

THE WORLD'S BEST SWIMMING POOLS

If you've ever wondered how the Four Seasons brand might do glamping, you'll find out here. The Four Seasons Tented Camp Golden Triangle is a safari-style lodge with ultra-luxe tents as accommodations, each with a hand-hammered soaking tub, an outdoor shower, and a deck with views into the jungle or out to the mountains beyond.

There is a second type of accommodation, and that's the extraordinary Explorer's Lodge, a two-bedroom villa with a private infinity pool that juts out over the hillside. Those in the tents will have to make do with a communal pool, but fortunately, it's a gorgeous natural-looking spot surrounded by boulders.

ASIA & THE MIDDLE EAST

| | **SIX SENSES YAO NOI** | 56 Moo 5, Tambol Koh Yao Noi, Amphur Koh Yao, Phang Nga, 82160 | **THAILAND** |

THE WORLD'S BEST SWIMMING POOLS

Set on the quiet island of Koh Yao Noi between Phuket and Krabi, Six Senses Yao Noi has a magnificent view of Phang Nga Bay and its limestone karsts. And it definitely takes advantage of that vista—a curved infinity pool crowns the property, prominently located at the very top of the hill onto which the resort is built. That alone is a fabulous spot to spend the afternoon, but the pools don't end there. Each of the 56 villas has its own pool, some nestled into gardens, others looking out to sea. And there's the white-sand beach for those who'd like to add the ocean to their to-swim list.

ASIA & THE MIDDLE EAST

At the Four Seasons Resort Chiang Mai, two pools blend in perfectly with the quiet ponds, verdant gardens, and terraced rice paddies that spill across the property. This halcyon resort is all about wellness, agriculture, and the arts: three pillars of the region's rural heritage. Visit the spa for a half-day Soulful Awakening program, plant your own rice seedlings, or take a pottery class—there's certainly no shortage of therapeutic activities. If you'd like to head into town for the day, Chiang Mai and its many temples are only a 30-minute drive away.

| | **FOUR SEASONS RESORT CHIANG MAI** | 502 Moo 1, Mae Rim-Samoeng Old Road, Chiang Mai, 50180 | THAILAND |

THE WORLD'S BEST SWIMMING POOLS

137 fourseasons.com/chiangmai

ASIA & THE MIDDLE EAST

FOUR SEASONS RESORT KOH SAMUI | 219 Moo 5, Angthong, Koh Samui, Surat Thani, 84140 | THAILAND

THE WORLD'S BEST SWIMMING POOLS

Everyone gets their own pool at the Four Seasons Resort Koh Samui, whether you're in a "modest" 1,108-square-foot Serenity Pool Villa or the grand five-bedroom residence, and each one of them has views of the sea. The whole resort is built on a hillside, so villas at the top have more of a jungle feel in a canopy of palms while villas at the bottom are right on the pristine beach. And don't worry, there's a communal infinity pool at the beach, too, alongside a restaurant and bar.

fourseasons.com/kohsamui

ASIA & THE MIDDLE EAST

| | **ST. REGIS LHASA RESORT** | No. 22, Jiangsu Road, Lhasa, Xizang, 850000 | TIBET (CHINA) |

Located within sightlines of Tibet's (China) imposing Potala Palace, a UNESCO World Heritage Site that was once the winter palace of the Dalai Lama, it's easy to look outward from the St. Regis Lhasa Resort. But turn inward and you'll find a heart of gold—in the form of a golden swimming pool in the Iridium Spa. Dubbed the Gold Energy Pool, it is indeed lined with thousands of 24-karat-gold tiles, creating an otherworldly effect. If you can tear yourself away from the mesmerizing sight, you can enjoy the rest of the hotel's amenities, including two fine-dining restaurants and a Potala-view bar.

ASIA & THE MIDDLE EAST

| | TITANIC MARDAN PALACE | Kundu Mah, Yaşar Sobutay Bulvari No: 450/1, Aksu, 07112 Antalya | TÜRKIYE |

THE WORLD'S BEST SWIMMING POOLS

It's not quite fair to simply call Titanic Mardan Palace an all-inclusive resort in Antalya, Türkiye. It's a true statement, but it doesn't fully capture the grandeur of the place. It's more of a palace resort, where sumptuous decor and endless activities abound—and it's all centered on a, well, titanic pool.

It spans more than 100,000 square feet and looks more like a lagoon than it does a pool. But then there are many other pools spread throughout the resort, from an indoor–outdoor saltwater pool to a more intimate heated outdoor pool.

titanic.com.tr/titanic-mardan-palace

ASIA & THE MIDDLE EAST

| | TITANIC GOLF DELUXE BELEK | Kadriye Mah, Üçkum Tepesi Mevkii Beşgöz Caddesi No: 72/1, Serik, 07525 Antalya | TÜRKIYE |

THE WORLD'S BEST SWIMMING POOLS

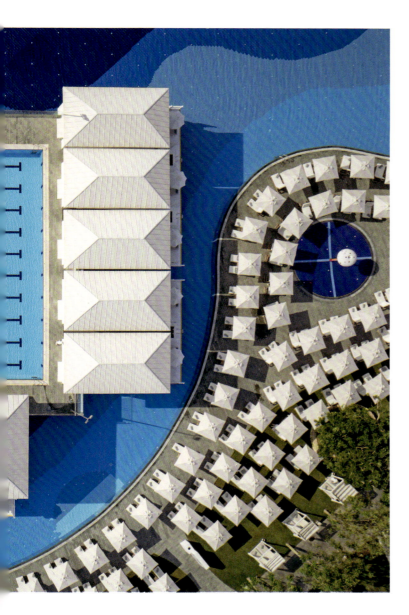

Golf might be the main attraction at the all-inclusive Titanic Golf Deluxe Belek resort just outside Antalya, Türkiye, but its sprawling pool complex is an eye-catcher, too. There are 10 pools here, including two indoor spots, adorned with everything from cabanas to waterslides to semi-submerged loungers to appeal to children and adults alike. The main outdoor pool is a lagoon-like free-form space; within it, you'll find a lap pool. Yes, a pool within a pool. There's also a heated hammam pool, a kids' activity pool, and a seawater pool, among many others.

titanic.com.tr/titanic-deluxe-golf-belek

ASIA & THE MIDDLE EAST

Pamukkale means "cotton castle" in Turkish, which is a fitting name for the milky-white calcium-laden travertine terraces you'll find in Türkiye's Denizli Province. The terraces are filled with mineral waters that have drawn visitors since the days of antiquity. In fact, the Ancient Greeks built the city of Hierapolis here as a spa town—the ruins of the city and the terraces have been designated the Hierapolis-Pamukkale UNESCO World Heritage Site. Some of the pools have been closed to swimming in order to protect the terraces, but a select few are open for a relaxing soak.

PAMUKKALE TRAVERTINES	Merkez, 20190 Pamukkale/Denizli	TÜRKIYE

146

ASIA & THE MIDDLE EAST

| | **PARK HYATT DUBAI** | Dubai Creek Club Street, Port Saeed, Dubai | UNITED ARAB EMIRATES |

THE WORLD'S BEST SWIMMING POOLS

The 223-room Park Hyatt Dubai, built along Dubai Creek, is a true resort, offering all the classic resort amenities like a golf course, a kids' club, a spa, and multiple restaurants and bars. Then there's the Amara Pool, an oasis-like watering hole surrounded by palm trees and anchored by whirlpools in its four corners, that welcomes both adults and children alike. The resort also has a man-made beach called Lagoon Beach, an adults-only spot with a lagoon-like infinity pool that's designed to appear to be part of the creek (which is actually a fairly large waterway).

hyatt.com/en-US/hotel/united-arab-emirates/park-hyatt-dubai/dxbph

ASIA & THE MIDDLE EAST

BURJ AL ARAB JUMEIRAH | Jumeirah Beach Road, Dubai | UNITED ARAB EMIRATES

THE WORLD'S BEST SWIMMING POOLS

As far as Dubai's many hotels go, few are as easily recognizable as the Burj Al Arab Jumeirah, a sail-shaped tower on a private island. The hotel brands itself a "seven-star hotel," and it absolutely goes over the top in terms of opulence. Take, for instance, the marvelous mosaics of the Talise Spa pools, where colorful tiles and punchy patterns abound. And those aren't even the primary pools! The two main pools are found on the Burj Al Arab Terrace, a multipurpose waterfront area that combines two pools, a restaurant, and plenty of cabanas and loungers in a beach-like setting. There's a freshwater pool for families and a curved saltwater infinity pool that abuts the sea.

ASIA & THE MIDDLE EAST

 | **TOPAS ECOLODGE** | Lech Dao Village, Thanh Binh Commune, Sapa District, Lao Cai Province | **VIETNAM**

THE WORLD'S BEST SWIMMING POOLS

Outside the town of Sapa in Vietnam, winding roads through rice terraces bring you to the hilltop Topas Ecolodge, a 49-room property with one standout pool. Or, rather, two of them! The dual infinity pools may look similar and have the same mountain views, but they're quite different in practice. The upper pool is heated (via an extremely energy-efficient system, I might add, in keeping with the property's sustainability goals) and is open to families, while the lower pool is refreshingly cool and is adults only. Off the upper pool, you'll find the Pool Bar serving up light bites, iced teas, and cocktails, as well as the Rice Spa.

ASIA & THE MIDDLE EAST

Ho Chi Minh City's Hôtel des Arts Saigon transports guests back to the 1930s with its French Indochina decor, but its scene is quite contemporary. Overnight guests, daytime visitors, and locals all flock to this property's stellar dining venues, and that includes the Social Club Rooftop Bar, perhaps best known for DJ sets post-sundown. In the same space as the bar, you'll find the hotel's saltwater rooftop pool, from which you can gaze out at the city skyline. While the bar is open to all, the pool is reserved for guests of the hotel.

HÔTEL DES ARTS SAIGON | 76-78 Nguyen Thi Minh Khai Street, District 3, Ho Chi Minh City, 70000 | VIETNAM

THE WORLD'S BEST SWIMMING POOLS

hoteldesartssaigon.com

ASIA & THE MIDDLE EAST

| | **JW MARRIOTT PHU QUOC EMERALD BAY** | Khem Beach, An Thoi Ward, Phu Quoc City, Kien Giang Province | VIETNAM |

Of all the themed hotels in the world, I find the theme of the JW Marriott Phu Quoc Emerald Bay to be unique. Its architect and interior designer, Bill Bensley, has conjured up an elaborate backstory to the resort: it was originally a late-19th-century French university, once abandoned and now restored. That history may be fabricated, but it adds a richness to the luxurious resort. As for the pools, there are three here. The Sand Pool is the largest, while the smaller Shell Pool and Sun Pool feature mosaics of their namesake motifs.

ASIA & THE MIDDLE EAST

| | **FOUR SEASONS RESORT THE NAM HAI, HOI AN** | Block Ha My Dong B, Dien Duong Ward, Dien Ban Town, Quang Nam Province | VIETNAM |

THE WORLD'S BEST SWIMMING POOLS

Take your pick from one of three main pools at the Four Seasons Resort The Nam Hai, Hoi An. Located in the center of the resort, the pools create a cascade of water features leading to the beach. The upper pool is a heated family-friendly pool; the middle pool is a narrow lap pool, and the lower pool is sized to meet Olympic qualifications. And these three options don't even take into account the nine Pool Villas, which each have their own infinity pool. Besides its pool (and the white-sand beach), this resort is known for its wellness offerings, including AntiGravity yoga, tai chi, and a crystal singing bowl experience.

fourseasons.com/hoian

ASIA & THE MIDDLE EAST

| **TIA WELLNESS RESORT** | 109 Vo Nguyen Giap Street, Khue My Ward, Ngu Hanh Son District, Danang City | VIETNAM |

THE WORLD'S BEST SWIMMING POOLS

Just 10 minutes from Da Nang and 30 minutes from UNESCO World Heritage Site of Hoi An, TIA Wellness resort is prime for day-tripping. But you might find it hard to pull yourself away from the boutique retreat. Wellness experiences are included in the rate, and you're entitled to up to 80 minutes of spa treatments per night of your stay, plus activities like tai chi, yoga, and breath work. When you're not in the spa, you'll want to lounge at the infinity-edge beachfront pool. Plus, each of its 87 villas also has a private plunge pool.

ASIA & THE MIDDLE EAST

 | **ZANNIER HOTELS BÃI SAN HÔ** | Hoa Thanh Hamlet, Xuan Cahn Commune, Song Cau District, Phu Yen Province | VIETNAM

THE WORLD'S BEST SWIMMING POOLS

At Bãi San Hô in southern Vietnam's Phu Yen province, 73 private villas—many with jaw-dropping pools—are spread across 242 acres of gardens. Their architecture is inspired by various traditional Vietnamese homes, from stilted fishermen's huts to mountain longhouses. There's also a communal 50-meter infinity pool with an adjacent pool bar, not to mention the secluded beach. It's easy to find ways to get in the water here, not least of which should include the hammams in the spa. And while you're there, book one of the therapies, which are guided by the five elements.

zannierhotels.com/baisanho/en

EUROPE

AMALIENBAD | Reumannplatz 23, 1100 Vienna | AUSTRIA

THE WORLD'S BEST SWIMMING POOLS

A rather nondescript building in Vienna hides within it one of the most dramatic public pools in Europe. With its Art Nouveau elements and Art Deco structure, Amalienbad in Vienna could undoubtedly be a set in a Wes Anderson film. Built between the two World Wars, this ornate municipal pool complex has it all. The main pool is set beneath a barrel-vaulted glass ceiling (the original, which was damaged during World War II, was retractable) and designed with lanes for lap swimming and platforms of varying heights for diving. Beyond this grand hall is a spa area with a thermal circuit, its walls decadently tiled in colorful mosaics.

EUROPE

| | **SUN GARDENS DUBROVNIK** | Na Moru 1, Orašac, 20235 Dubrovnik | CROATIA |

THE WORLD'S BEST SWIMMING POOLS

Just seven miles north of Dubrovnik, Sun Gardens is a peaceful, family-friendly beach retreat with views of the Adriatic Sea. When you're not down at the pebble beach, you can spend time lounging at the resort's three lovely pools, two of which have children's pools attached, and the third of which is adults only. There's also an indoor pool at the spa, as well as a thermal circuit. During the summer, the hotel offers a boat shuttle to Dubrovnik, but you truly don't ever need to leave the resort—there are 15 bars and restaurants here to occupy your time beyond sunning and bathing.

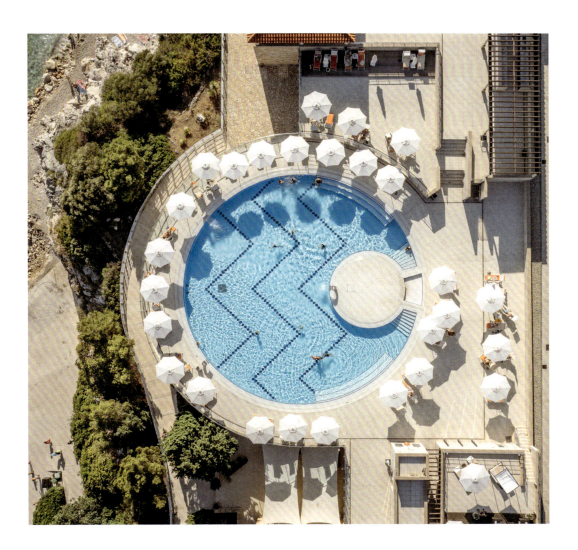

169   dubrovniksungardens.com

EUROPE

 | **MANON LES SUITES** | Gyldenløvesgade 19, 1600 Copenhagen V | **DENMARK**

THE WORLD'S BEST SWIMMING POOLS

You'd be forgiven if you thought you were in Bali at this extraordinary indoor swimming pool. Known as the Junglefish Pool, this watering hole is set in an atrium overflowing with greenery and accented by charming fish light fixtures. But it's not in Bali—it's in Copenhagen, at the Manon Les Suites hotel. Photogenic pool aside, the boutique hotel has an ideal location that makes it a worthwhile stay, just a 10-minute walk from Tivoli Gardens and a 15-minute walk from the main train station. There's also a rooftop lounge and sauna for a more Scandinavian touch.

guldsmedenhotels.com/manon-les-suites

EUROPE

ROYAL CHAMPAGNE HOTEL & SPA

9 Rue de la République, Champillon, Marne, 51160

FRANCE

To be fully transparent, if you're staying at the Royal Champagne Hotel & Spa, you're probably here for the bubbly, not the pool. And it's completely understandable. The gastronomic experience at this luxury hotel in the Marne Valley of France's Champagne region is on another level, between the Michelin-starred restaurant Le Royal, the bistro Le Bellevue, and the Abysse Bar. (It's also worth noting the afternoon tea service, which you should absolutely pair with Champagne.) But don't sleep on the spa experience, which includes both indoor and outdoor pools, permitting swimming all year round. Both have spectacular vineyard views.

EUROPE

**HÔTEL CRILLON
LE BRAVE**

Place de l'Eglise,
Crillon-le-Brave,
Vaucluse, 84410

FRANCE

THE WORLD'S BEST SWIMMING POOLS

Disconnect at Hôtel Crillon Le Brave, a resort comprising a number of 17th-century and 18th-century buildings in a Provençal village in the foothills of Mont Ventoux. It's all about meandering the cobblestoned alleyways, delighting in French cuisine, and being pampered at the spa, which is housed in the former stables. Throw in an afternoon lounging by the green-tiled infinity pool and gazing out at the panorama in front of you, and you've got yourself a relaxing getaway. If you feel the need for a little activity, rent one of the property's bikes and go for a ride.

EUROPE

HÔTEL LES ROCHES ROUGES | 90 Boulevard de la 36ème Division du Texas, Saint-Raphaël, Côte d'Azur, 83530 | FRANCE

THE WORLD'S BEST SWIMMING POOLS

The pinnacle of French Riviera chic, Hôtel Les Roches Rouges in Saint-Raphaël oozes mid-century charm. It was, after all, built in the 1950s—but as a little motel, not a design star. It's matured over the years to become an utterly stylish stay. Beyond its dapper decor, the hotel stands out for its marvelous saltwater pool, built into the rocks along the edge of the sea. If the sea spray isn't suitable for you, there's also a lap pool built onto a terrace. For lunch, grab an aperitif and a Provençal dish like pissaladière from the pool bar, and for dinner, head inside to the Michelin-starred Récif.

beaumier.com/en/properties/les-roches-rouges-hotel

EUROPE

| | SHANGRI-LA PARIS | 10 Avenue d'Iéna, Paris, 75116 | FRANCE |

THE WORLD'S BEST SWIMMING POOLS

You'd hardly know you were in the center of Paris during a swim at the Shangri-La Paris's Chi Spa pool. That all changes when you head upstairs—many of the rooms have Eiffel Tower views, sometimes even from the tub. The 17-meter-long pool feels like a contemporary Grecian sanctuary with mosaics lining the floor and columns supporting the ceiling (which is painted to look like the sky, I might add). The space has plenty of natural light let in through floor-to-ceiling windows facing a terrace garden. If you're not a guest here, you can book a day pass, and if you happen to live in Paris, you can even become a spa member.

EUROPE

If you're willing to take a bit of a hike through the scenic Cavu Valley, some 30 minutes outside Porto-Vecchio, you'll find natural swimming pools tucked between granite boulders that are fed by the Cavu River. Wear good shoes if you plan on making the trek, as the rocks can be slippery and the terrain is uneven. The pools are not so remote, though, that there are no facilities here—there's a lovely Corsican restaurant called Les 3 Piscines, and it's a perfect spot to fuel up after a hike and a swim.

	PISCINES NATURELLES DE CAVU	Cavu River, D168A 20144, Zonza, Corsica	**FRANCE**

EUROPE

LA PISCINE DE BON-SECOURS | Place du Guet Intra-Muros, Saint-Malo, Brittany | FRANCE

THE WORLD'S BEST SWIMMING POOLS

The Brittany region of France has hundreds of miles of coastline, including many beaches, but one of the standouts—at least in terms of pools—is the Plage de Bon-Secours in Saint-Malo. The beach beneath the city's ramparts is renowned for its large sea pool, which was built in the 1930s to provide beachgoers a place to swim when the tide went out. (At low tide, the water retreats enough for you to walk to the nearby islands.) The concrete barrier that forms the edge of the pool has a three-tier diving platform on its far side for those willing to swim out to it.

saint-malo-tourisme.co.uk/offers/plage-de-bon-secours-saint-malo-en-3646045

EUROPE

TROPICAL ISLANDS RESORT | Tropical-Islands-Allee 1, Krausnick, 15910 | GERMANY

THE WORLD'S BEST SWIMMING POOLS

What do you do with a giant decommissioned airship hangar? Turn it into an indoor waterpark, of course. That's precisely what happened in Krausnick, Germany, about an hour's drive south of Berlin. Tropical Islands Resort is the closest thing to a tropical paradise in Germany, with dozens of attractions, shops, restaurants, and accommodations. Inside the hangar are several themed areas with different water attractions, including a pool that's three times the size of an Olympic pool. There's also an outdoor extension that's open year-round, where you'll find a surf simulator and the longest whitewater channel in Germany.

tropical-islands.de/en

EUROPE

Where to begin with the pools at Calilo, an acronym for "create a life you can fall in love with"? There are many on the independent resort, a hilly, secluded 1,000-acre property on the island of Ios. Most are private, attached to many of the 30 individually designed suites—some might take the shape of a heart, while others are shaded by a roof from which hangs a swinging daybed. Yet others still have meandering pathways that separate the pool into sections. There is a main pool down at the beach, a sprawling, curving body of water, at the center of which is a towering statue, one of many works of art at Calilo.

 | **CALILO** | Papas Beach, Ios, Aegean Islands, 840 01 | **GREECE**

THE WORLD'S BEST SWIMMING POOLS

EUROPE

 ASTARTE SUITES | Caldera-Akrotiri, Santorini, Aegean Islands, 847 03 | GREECE

THE WORLD'S BEST SWIMMING POOLS

Santorini's famous vistas of the Aegean Sea are best taken in from a pool. At Astarte Suites in Akrotiri, a shared infinity pool provides those views, as do the private pools in some of the 13 accommodations. Each suite is unique, with a different layout—if I were you, I'd go for the Cave Pool Suite, which, as its name suggests, has a small private pool surrounded by a whitewashed man-made "cave." It's particularly stunning at night, when the blue light from the pool illuminates the domed overhang.

astartesuites.gr/en

EUROPE

KATIKIES CHROMATA | Imerovigli, Santorini, Aegean Islands, 847 00 | GREECE

The little village of Imerovigli, known as the "Balcony on the Aegean," is home to Katikies Chromata, a charming cliffside cave hotel built into the volcanic rock of Santorini. The decor here is minimalist—pretty much everything is white, save for a red flower here and there, some pale-blue trim on the pillows, and the yellow-striped pool towels—and that allows the view to shine. There's a communal infinity pool looking out across the sea for those staying in pool-less suites, but it's worth splurging for a private plunge pool if you can.

EUROPE

| | CANAVES OIA SUITES, A CANAVES COLLECTION HOTEL | Main Street, Oia, Santorini, Aegean Islands, 847 02 | GREECE |

THE WORLD'S BEST SWIMMING POOLS

Cycladic architecture and contemporary design meld seamlessly at Canaves Oia Suites, an iconic property in the village of Oia. It certainly checks all the Santorini boxes: whitewashed walls, caldera views from a cliffside perch, and, of course, azure infinity pools. The communal pool is lined with partially submerged loungers, which is a welcome respite from the heat of summer. Lean over the edge of the pool if you dare to see the sparkling water below. Every suite and villa here has a private pool, too, but they vary in layout. The River Pool Suite has a tunnel-like pool that opens up to an infinity edge, while the Executive Suite with Cave Pool has, you guessed it, a cave pool.

EUROPE

 GIOLA LAGOON | Thassos, Aegean Islands | GREECE

THE WORLD'S BEST SWIMMING POOLS

At the edge of the Giola Lagoon on Greece's Thassos Island is a teardrop-shaped natural pool that calls to both daredevils and photographers. For adrenaline seekers, there's the allure of jumping from the cliffs surrounding the pool into its clear-blue waters. For photographers, getting a shot of the action—or an overhead shot via drone—is the goal. Giola is also known as "the Tear of Aphrodite," as legend has it Zeus created the pool for his daughter Aphrodite to swim in. Thassos also has another connection to Greek mythology: it's thought to be the home of the Sirens.

EUROPE

| | **ANDRONIS ARCADIA** | Oia, Santorini, Aegean Islands, 847 02 | GREECE |

THE WORLD'S BEST SWIMMING POOLS

Named after the home of the Greek god Pan, Andronis Arcadia is a picturesque resort in Oia on Santorini. Each of its more than 50 guest accommodations is a suite or a villa done up in traditional whitewashed architecture and elegant nature-inspired decor, and every one has a private heated plunge pool. If that weren't enough, there are three shared pools across the property: the infinity pool flanked by a casual restaurant and bar, the beach club-esque Grande Pool with sun beds and evening DJ sets, and the thermal circuit Kneipp pools in the spa.

EUROPE

| | **CANAVES EPITOME, A CANAVES COLLECTION RESORT** | Main Street, Oia, Santorini, Aegean Islands, 847 02 | GREECE |

THE WORLD'S BEST SWIMMING POOLS

If you've already stayed in a hotel with the traditional whitewashed walls that are so prevalent in Santorini and are looking for a change of scenery, Canaves Epitome is the resort for you. Here, buildings are made of rough-hewn gray volcanic stone, though there are still white walls to be found throughout. The accommodations, however, don't have the curved cave walls of other Santorini hotels—they're rectilinear, though they do have arched windows that look out to the Aegean Sea. Each has a private plunge pool, and there are two sleek infinity pools for guests to share.

canaves.com/canaves-oia-epitome

EUROPE

CRETAN MALIA PARK Malia, Crete, 700 07 GREECE

A former campsite turned elegant eco resort, Cretan Malia Park is defined by several pools across its gardened grounds. The heated Main Swimming Pool is surrounded by a deck with sun beds; the River Pool, the largest on the property, winds its way through the property, past bungalows with direct pool access, alongside restaurants, and beneath a footbridge; and the Paddling Pool is a shallow spot for children. You could easily spend your whole stay switching between the three, but be sure to make time for the beach, too.

EUROPE

GELLÉRT THERMAL BATH | Kelenhegyi út 2, Budapest, 1114 | HUNGARY

THE WORLD'S BEST SWIMMING POOLS

Though the history records show that people have been enjoying the waters at Gellért Thermal Bath since the 15th century, the elaborate Art Nouveau bathhouse that exists today opened in 1918, with expansions in 1927 and 1934. Inside are various thermal pools, each housed in a highly ornamental space adorned with details like shimmering metallic mosaics and stained-glass windows. And there are outdoor pools, too, as well as saunas, a spa offering massages and pedicures, and a shop selling homemade soaps. If you've forgotten your bathing suit and towel, don't fret—you can rent them from the pool.

gellertbath.hu

EUROPE

Budapest's Széchenyi Baths make most of the "must-visit" lists written about the city, and that's not too much of a surprise. The spa baths are part of an ancient tradition of soaking in the natural waters here—the Romans, who built the city of Aquincum on these lands, had thermal baths. Today, it's not just about the waters, which can be enjoyed in both smaller indoor pools and three giant outdoor ones. It's also about the ornate yellow building by Győző Czigler, erected in the early 20th century. Be forewarned that it can get crowded here, especially during the spa parties on summer nights.

	SZÉCHENYI BATHS	Állatkerti körút 9-11, Budapest, 1146	**HUNGARY**

THE WORLD'S BEST SWIMMING POOLS

szechenyibath.hu

EUROPE

| | ION ADVENTURE HOTEL | Nesjavellir vid Thingvallavatn, Selfoss, 801 | ICELAND |

THE WORLD'S BEST SWIMMING POOLS

The perfect base camp for excursions into UNESCO World Heritage Site Thingvellir National Park—I personally recommend snorkeling or scuba diving at Silfra, a submerged fissure between the North American and Eurasian tectonic plates—ION Adventure Hotel has a rugged yet luxe spirit.

The hotel is something of a hybrid. A formerly abandoned inn metamorphoses into a starkly modern concrete structure elevated by thick concrete stilts, and it's in this undercarriage that you'll find the geothermally heated pool. It's part of the lava spa, where you can relax after a long day of activities in Thingvellir.

213   ionadventure.ioniceland.is

EUROPE

 | **ELEVEN DEPLAR FARM** | Fljot 570, Skagafjörður | ICELAND

THE WORLD'S BEST SWIMMING POOLS

Once a sheep farm, now a heli-skiing and salmon-fishing resort, Deplar Farm is unlike any other hotel in Iceland. It's located on the northern Troll Peninsula, a particularly snowy spot; hence the heli-skiing. And while it might be out in the middle of nowhere, it provides all the luxuries one might need during their stay. That includes a hot spring-esque outdoor pool heated to a balmy 99 degrees Fahrenheit, bordering on hot tub territory. All the better on winter nights when you're waiting for the northern lights to appear.

elevenexperience.com/deplar-farm-iceland-winter

EUROPE

 | **SELJAVALLALAUG** | Off Route 242 in South Iceland | ICELAND

THE WORLD'S BEST SWIMMING POOLS

Iceland has a robust bathing culture—that is, most towns have a public pool where residents gather for swimming, socializing, and soaking. In fact, all Icelanders must take swimming lessons into their teenage years. But that was not always the case. Back in 1923, a man by the name of Björn Andrésson built the Seljavallalaug pool to teach the residents of the Seljavellir fishing community how to swim, as many fishermen lacked the skill. Today, there's a newer pool in town, but visitors often trek 20 minutes along the river to the old spot for its unparalleled scenery. Though you can hop into this geothermally heated pool, take note that it's cleaned only once a year— it might be more photogenic than it is hygienic.

EUROPE

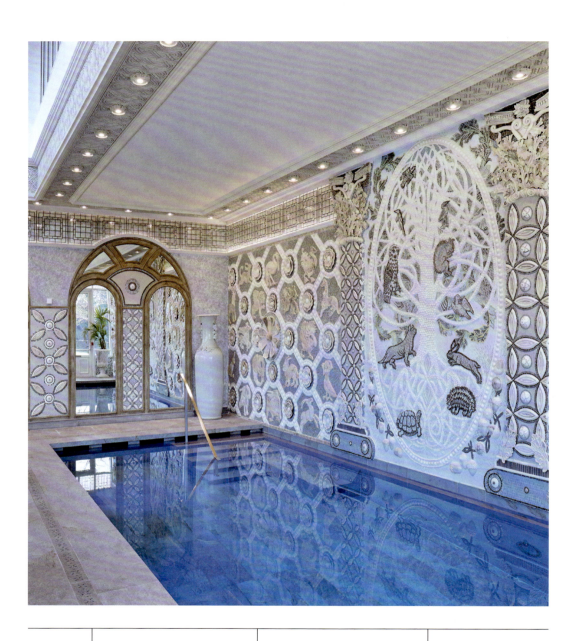

ASHFORD CASTLE | Ashford Castle Drive, Cong, County Mayo, F31 CA48 | IRELAND

Breathtaking. There's no other word for the relaxation pool at the spa at Ashford Castle. The bright and airy space, furnished with ornate loungers and glittering chandeliers, is anchored by an exquisite mural by South African artist Jane du Rand. It depicts the Tree of Life from Celtic mythology, as well as local Irish flora, fauna, and motifs. Ashford Castle is undoubtedly one of the best hotels in all of Ireland, housed in a 13th-century stone castle on Lough Corrib, an hour outside of Galway. Activities here include classic manor fun like falconry, fishing, and horseback riding.

EUROPE

There are many grand hotels on Lake Como, but perhaps none more grand than the Grand Hotel Tremezzo. Opened in 1910, the Art Nouveau palazzo proudly faces the shimmering lake and looks out onto its magnificent floating pool known as WOW!, or Water-On-The-Water. Talk about maximizing space! But that's just one of the hotel's pools: the Flowers Pool is tucked away in the gardens, and there's a third one in the T Spa. That last pool is particularly lovely, as it's an indoor infinity pool that faces the lake. Appropriately, it's called the Infinity Pool.

| | **GRAND HOTEL TREMEZZO** | Via Regina, 8, 22016 Tremezzina, Como | ITALY |

THE WORLD'S BEST SWIMMING POOLS

grandhoteltremezzo.com/en/home

EUROPE

ALPIN PANORAMA HOTEL HUBERTUS | Via Furcia, 5, 39030 Sorafurcia, Valdaora, South Tyrol | ITALY

THE WORLD'S BEST SWIMMING POOLS

This pool in Italy's Dolomites takes the concept of an infinity pool to new heights. The 25-meter-long Sky Pool at Alpin Panorama Hotel Hubertus is cantilevered over mountain meadows, jutting out into the valley below. It also has a glass window at the bottom to better showcase its height above the ground. Yet this pool wasn't enough for the hotel—it has five more on its grounds: a panoramic pool, a relaxation pool, a saltwater pool, a whirlpool, and an indoor pool. Two of the pools are heated to 91 degrees Fahrenheit, while the relaxation pool and whirlpool are extra warm at 99 degrees, and the indoor pool is a touch cooler at 86 degrees.

hotel-hubertus.com/en

EUROPE

 | **IL SERENO** | Via Torrazza, 10, 22020 Torno, Como | ITALY

While most of Lake Como's luxury hotels are housed in palazzos, Il Sereno bucks the trend—it's a new build that embraces its contemporaneity. Designer Patricia Urquiola is behind the modernist interiors, which focus on earthy hues and natural materials. Its pool, however, is a bit more in the style of its neighbors. It's built into a wood deck along the shoreline, though it isn't floating as some others are, and it's lined with green loungers and tented sun beds. The spa is also located on the lakefront in a former boathouse.

EUROPE

	MONASTERO SANTA ROSA HOTEL & SPA	Via Roma, 2, 84010 Conca dei Marini, Salerno, Campania	ITALY

THE WORLD'S BEST SWIMMING POOLS

Formerly a 17th-century convent, now a luxury hotel, the Monastero Santa Rosa Hotel & Spa puts the Amalfi Coast's cliffs to good use, planting terraced gardens along the rocky outcrops and building an infinity pool right at the edge of a precipice. There are just 20 rooms and suites at the boutique property, as well as a Michelin-starred restaurant and a spa with a full thermal suite. Monastero Santa Rosa is located some three miles outside of the town of Amalfi—which means it has plenty of peace and quiet. For those looking to go into town, the hotel provides a free shuttle.

monasterosantarosa.com

EUROPE

**ROCCA DELLE
TRE CONTRADE**

Via Dogana, 95010 Santa
Venerina, Catania, Sicily

ITALY

THE WORLD'S BEST SWIMMING POOLS

Rocca delle Tre Contrade might just be Sicily's most extraordinary accommodation. A formerly derelict villa on a Sicilian hillside between the sea and Mount Etna has been transformed into a 12-bedroom private retreat that's bookable by the general public. The property is fully staffed for your stay—the team includes a Sicilian private chef who will create magnificent meals for you—and includes amenities like a tennis court, access to Belmond Villa Sant'Andrea's lido on the beach at Mazzarò, and, of course, a 25-meter infinity pool that can be heated for your comfort (or left cool for an invigorating plunge).

EUROPE

GROTTA DELLA POESIA | Strada Statale San Cataldo, 73026 Roca Vecchia, Lecce, Apulia | ITALY

THE WORLD'S BEST SWIMMING POOLS

The Grotta della Poesia, or the "Cave of Poetry," is a natural swimming pool found on the archeological site of Roca Vecchia, located between the city of Lecce and the town of Otranto. While many visitors come for the ruins found throughout the site, others certainly come for the Grotta della Poesia—some to swim, some to cliff jump, some just to take in its beauty. It was formerly a sea cave, but years of erosion led to the collapse of the stone above it, revealing its waters to the sky.

EUROPE

Just as Venice is known for its canals, Hotel Cipriani, a Belmond Hotel, is known for its pool—it's the only one in the city center. And it's an extremely impressive pool at that. Fully Olympic-sized, the pool is filled with filtered and heated salt water, and it's surrounded by loungers, umbrellas, and a garden. Order a light lunch at Il Porticciolo after a swim, or sip Aperol spritzes or bellinis from the comfort of your lounger. It's the best way to beat the heat during a summer vacation in Venice.

| | **HOTEL CIPRIANI, A BELMOND HOTEL** | Giudecca, 10, 30133 Venice | ITALY |

THE WORLD'S BEST SWIMMING POOLS

235 belmond.com/hotels/europe/italy/venice/belmond-hotel-cipriani

THE WORLD'S BEST SWIMMING POOLS

EUROPE

| | **LE CASCATE DEL MULINO** | Strada Vicinale Molino del Bagno, 9/a, 58014 Saturnia, Grosseto, Tuscany | **ITALY** |

THE WORLD'S BEST SWIMMING POOLS

When you picture Tuscany, rolling hills covered by vineyards and historic villages likely come to mind. But the region is also known for its hot springs, perhaps none more famous than Le Cascate del Mulino. Located near the village of Saturnia, these thermal springs cascade down a hillside, forming white-rimmed terraced pools filled with baby-blue water that's naturally heated to 99.5 degrees Fahrenheit. Perhaps unsurprisingly, these beautiful hot springs have drawn visitors looking for a soothing soak for millennia. You can take a dip all year round, but be forewarned that these pools can get quite crowded during peak tourist season, especially on weekends.

EUROPE

| | **MANDARIN ORIENTAL, LAGO DI COMO** | Via Caronti, 69, 22020 Blevio, Como | **ITALY** |

THE WORLD'S BEST SWIMMING POOLS

The elegant Mandarin Oriental, Lago di Como, is housed in a 19th-century palazzo tucked into botanical gardens that looks as if it could be a set piece in a romantic film or perhaps an opera. It shouldn't be too surprising, then, that an opera star once called this her home. The property is a luxe hotel now, though, with guests residing in 75 opulent suites. Backed by a teak deck, the outdoor infinity pool here appears to float on Lake Como, but it's only an effective illusion. There's also a cave-like indoor pool in the spa, while the exclusive Panoramic Suite has its own infinity pool built into the hillside.

mandarinoriental.com/en/lake-como/blevio/stay

EUROPE

Flooded quarries don't make for the best pools, as inviting as they might seem—they can be quite hazardous to swimmers. But a former limestone quarry in Zakrzówek Park near the city center of Krakow is a different story. There are five suspended pools of varying depths built into the quarry lake, surrounded and connected by wooden platforms for sunbathing. The pools are staffed by lifeguards, and they're cleaned weekly to maintain good hygiene. While you can still swim in the lake if you so choose, you'll have to do so at your own risk.

| | **ZAKRZÓWEK PARK POOLS** | Zakrzówek Park, Krakow | **POLAND** |

242

THE WORLD'S BEST SWIMMING POOLS

EUROPE

ALBATROZ BEACH & YACHT CLUB | Quinta Dr. Américo Durão, Sítio da Terça, Santa Cruz, Madeira | PORTUGAL

THE WORLD'S BEST SWIMMING POOLS

There are just 20 rooms at the Albatroz Beach & Yacht Club, a boutique property tucked between the runway of Madeiria's Funchal Airport and the Atlantic Ocean. There are three pools here, the most striking of which is an asymmetrical saltwater pool at sea level, built atop a small rocky outcrop at the base of the seaside cliffs. But there's another saltwater pool down here, as well as a cliff-top freshwater pool with hot tubs—there are quite a few options for such a small resort! Other amenities include a turf tennis court, a spa and sauna, a gym, and a restaurant.

albatrozhotel.com/en

EUROPE

 DÁ LICENÇA | Outeiro das Freiras – Santo Estêvão, Alentejo, 7100-580 | PORTUGAL

246

THE WORLD'S BEST SWIMMING POOLS

In Portugal's wine-producing Alentejo region, you'll find Dá Licença, a beautifully renovated centuries-old farmhouse on a 300-acre estate filled with olive groves and striking marble formations. Though the property may be historic, the renovations have expertly brought the six suites and shared spaces into the contemporary day, highlighting the region's famed pink marble. The crown jewel of Dá Licença is the unique 15-meter circular pool, inspired by the celestial beauty of the moon and stars. Two suites also have their own pools: My Pool and Sky Pool.

· dalicenca.pt/en

EUROPE

VENTOZELO HOTEL & QUINTA

Quinta de Ventozelo, São João da Pesqueira, Ervedosa do Douro, 5130-135

PORTUGAL

THE WORLD'S BEST SWIMMING POOLS

A true quinta, or wine estate and farm, in Portugal's Douro Valley, Ventozelo has just 29 rooms spread across its sprawling, nearly 1,000-acre grounds—it's one of the oldest and largest farms in the region, and it's still a working farm today. Staying here as a guest allows you to dive headfirst into viticulture and agriculture, all the while staying in well-appointed accommodations. Some of the seven buildings that house the guest rooms have pools that overlook the vineyard-covered hills, and there's a main infinity pool for all to share.

249   hotel.quintadeventozelo.pt

EUROPE

| | PENHA LONGA RESORT | Quinta da Penha Longa, Estrada da Lagoa Azul, Linhó, Sintra, 2714-511 | PORTUGAL |

THE WORLD'S BEST SWIMMING POOLS

There's plenty to do at Penha Longa Resort, a fabulous retreat within a 545-acre national park in Portugal's Sintra Mountains. Perhaps the biggest draw is a championship 18-hole golf course designed by Robert Trent Jones Jr. Or maybe it's the eight restaurants, three of which have been awarded Michelin stars. Or could it be the Asian-inspired spa? It's likely the combination of all the resort's activities, and that includes its beautiful infinity pool that faces the mountains—plus the two other outdoor pools, and the indoor pool in the spa.

penhalonga.com/en

EUROPE

 | **CAMPO DE ARROZ** | Lagoa Formosa, Carvalhal, Alentejo, 7570-782 | PORTUGAL

THE WORLD'S BEST SWIMMING POOLS

The sleepy seaside village of Comporta in Portugal has become something of an international hot spot for interior design, drawing in well-heeled vacationers who have purchased their own properties there. If buying a vacation home isn't in your budget, don't fret—there are many rentals here, too, including Campo de Arroz, a two-house complex just a 15-minute drive from the center of town, in the village of Lagoa Formosa. Accommodating up to 10 people, the property has a scenic infinity pool overlooking the rice paddies for which it's named.

alma-da-comporta.com/houses/campo-de-arroz

EUROPE

| | PORTO MONIZ NATURAL SWIMMING POOLS | Porto Moniz, northwestern coast of Madeira Island | PORTUGAL |

THE WORLD'S BEST SWIMMING POOLS

Thanks to the volcanic geology of Madeira, the rocky coastline of the island is filled with natural pools—some of the best of which are found in Porto Moniz. There are multiple spots here that cater to different types of swimmers. The Cachalote natural swimming pools, located near the town's main gate, meander through volcanic rocks and are a picturesque way to enjoy the blue-green water. Then there are the Velhas natural swimming pools, which have been modified for something of an easier swimming experience—there are concrete terraces interspersed throughout the volcanic rocks, with steps down into the pools. Both pool destinations are worthy of a swim, but if you have kids, opt for the latter.

portomoniz.pt/en/visit/points-interest/beaches

EUROPE

It's not often that swimming pools are associated with world-famous architects, but the tidal pools of Leça da Palmeira were designed by a Portuguese legend. Pritzker Prize–winning architect Álvaro Siza Vieira completed these modernist pools in 1966—they are one of his early projects, along with the Boa Nova Tea House just down the road—creating two pools at the edge of the ocean that are refreshed with salt water at each high tide. It was his intention to blend artifice, in the form of the blunt concrete structures, with the natural rocky landscape.

| | **TIDAL POOLS OF LEÇA DA PALMEIRA** | Matosinhos e Leça da Palmeira, Porto | **PORTUGAL** |

256

THE WORLD'S BEST SWIMMING POOLS

matosinhosport.pt/piscinas/piscinas/piscina-das-mares

EUROPE

MANDARIN ORIENTAL, BARCELONA | Passeig de Gràcia, 38-40, 08007 Barcelona | SPAIN

THE WORLD'S BEST SWIMMING POOLS

The two pools at the elegant Mandarin Oriental, Barcelona, couldn't be more different. On the rooftop, a hedge-lined pool accents a terrace with views of the city skyline; in the same space is the Terrat restaurant and bar, which serves Peruvian bites and cocktails. Here, you can take a personalized yoga lesson or guided meditation session. Then in the subterranean spa, you'll find a moody, emerald space with an inky pool—it's certainly one of the more unique swimming experiences out there. Even if you don't want to take a dip, it's worth going for the photo alone.

mandarinoriental.com/en/barcelona/passeig-de-gracia

EUROPE

There's perhaps no hotel on Mallorca that feels more secluded than Cap Rocat, set in a former 19th-century military fortress that once guarded the Bay of Palma and is now a national monument. It's set into a nature reserve, so while it's only 20 minutes from downtown Palma, it feels a world away. There are several pools here, including a large outdoor infinity pool and a seawater pool in the spa, but some of the best are the private plunge pools attached to six of the 26 suites, which are built into the cliffside and have top ocean views.

| | **CAP ROCAT** | Carretera d'enderrocat, s/n, 07609 Cala Blava, Mallorca, Balearic Islands | **SPAIN** |

THE WORLD'S BEST SWIMMING POOLS

EUROPE

CHARCO DE LA LAJA | San Juan de la Rambla, Tenerife, Canary Islands | SPAIN

THE WORLD'S BEST SWIMMING POOLS

The volcanic island of Tenerife in Spain's Canary Islands is lined with naturally formed rock pools along the ocean's edge, but one of the most frequently visited is Charco de la Laja, next to the town of San Juan de la Rambla. Descend a rocky path to find a clear-blue pool among the jagged rocks—just be careful that you don't slip. And as with any rock pool, be cognizant of the tide and the weather! It's not unusual for waves to splash over the rock wall into this pool.

sanjuandelarambla.es/areas-municipales/area-de-turismo/charco-de-la-laja

EUROPE

| **LAS SALINAS DE AGAETE** | Calle el Muelle, 17, Agaete, Las Palmas, Canary Islands | SPAIN |

THE WORLD'S BEST SWIMMING POOLS

This trio of natural rock pools is said to resemble a submerged castle, thanks to the battlement-like posts lining their rims (they're here to help break any waves that crash into the pools). A popular swimming spot in the summertime, these pools are connected by underwater tunnels that you can swim through, if you're careful. And because they're connected to the sea, you never know if some local aquatic wildlife might end up in the pools, too. They're located just a five-minute walk from the harbor village Puerto de las Nieves, though there's also a small parking lot next to the pools if you drive.

EUROPE

| | **HOTEL VILLA HONEGG** | Honegg, 6373 Ennetbürgen, Lucerne | SWITZERLAND |

THE WORLD'S BEST SWIMMING POOLS

There are just 23 rooms at this Art Nouveau–style villa built into the hills above Lake Lucerne in 1905. From its vantage point, it provides spectacular lake and mountain views. While gastronomy and access to hiking and mountain biking trails are two of the many reasons guests love this property, another standout is its wellness offerings, in particular, the outdoor infinity pool heated to 93.2 degrees Fahrenheit. If you're not staying at the hotel, you can book a day pass to the spa facilities and the pool, availability permitting.

villa-honegg.ch

EUROPE

BÜRGENSTOCK RESORT LAKE LUCERNE | Obbürgen, 6363 Stansstad, Lucerne | SWITZERLAND

THE WORLD'S BEST SWIMMING POOLS

Pools abound at Bürgenstock Resort, a sprawling hotel, spa, and residential complex built onto a ridge some 1,640 feet above Switzerland's Lake Lucerne in 1873. It's impossible to choose a favorite, between the outdoor infinity pool heated to 95 degrees Fahrenheit and the elegant indoor pool with floor-to-ceiling windows to take in the elevated views. There are also many wellness-oriented pools, like a salt pool and an (unheated) lake-water pool. And there's even a Hollywood pool, so named for the Hollywood A-listers who have vacationed (and swum) here, from Audrey Hepburn to Sophia Loren.

burgenstockresort.com

EUROPE

Located in the spa town of Vals, Switzerland, 7132 Hotel is a temple for architecture. The luxury hotel tapped Japanese architects Tadao Ando and Kengo Kuma, American architect Thom Mayne, and Swiss architect Peter Zumthor to conceive spaces in a former mid-century hotel complex to complement Zumthor's other work (and the star of the show, at least for this book): the 7132 Thermal Baths. Mineral water from the St. Peter spring, naturally heated to 86 degrees Fahrenheit, flows through this labyrinthine spa facility built from 60,000 stacked slabs of Vals quartzite.

| | **7132 THERMAL BATHS** | 7132 Vals, Graubünden | SWITZERLAND |

EUROPE

| **TUNNELS BEACHES** | Bath Place, Ilfracombe, Devon, EX34 8AN | **UNITED KINGDOM** |

Back in the 1820s when bathing was considered a medical treatment for many ailments, Ilfracombe Sea Bathing Company hired miners to hand-carve tunnels to connect the town of Ilfracombe to three bathing pools by the sea. Today, you can still traverse those tunnels to swim in one of the tidal pools, though you may find the water to be a touch cold. Tunnels Beaches is also a popular wedding venue for those looking to be married by the sea—the setting certainly makes for stunning photography, particularly at sunset.

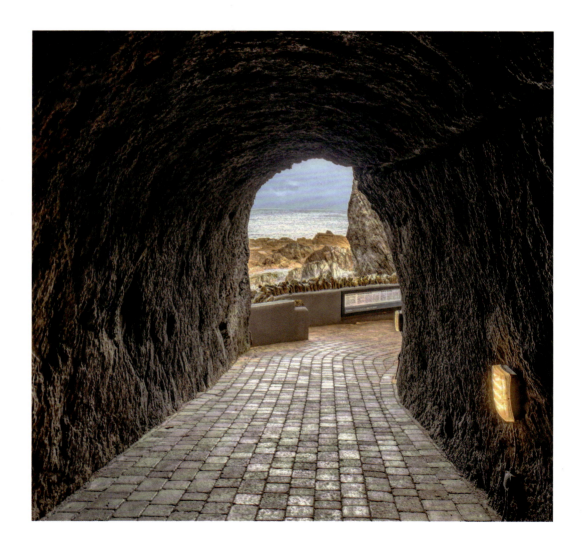

EUROPE

JUBILEE POOL | Battery Road, Penzance, Cornwall, TR18 4FF | **UNITED KINGDOM**

The British have a long tradition of swimming in saltwater lidos, and though many of the pools no longer exist, there are several that still welcome swimmers today. Jubilee Pool in Penzance, opened in 1935, is one of the finest surviving examples in operation today, thanks to its Art Deco architecture—and the fact that it's the largest pool in the country. Though damage from storms and diminishing visitor numbers once threatened the pool, renovations have revitalized the facility. Today there are three pools here: a sprawling main pool, a children's pool, and a geothermically heated pool, the latter of which is open year-round.

jubileepool.co.uk

EUROPE

TINSIDE LIDO | Hoe Road, Plymouth, Devon, PL1 2AA | **UNITED KINGDOM**

Tinside Lido's tale follows a familiar storyline. Built in 1935 in the Art Deco style, the 55-meter seawater pool in Plymouth experienced a rise and fall throughout its life, peaking during the heyday of the lido tradition but ultimately closing due to waning popularity and neglect in 1992. But thanks to ardent local support, the facility was added to the National Heritage List for England and has since been restored to its original grandeur. The pool, anchored by a fountain in the center of its semicircular shape, is now open in the summertime for public use.

EUROPE

EMBASSY GARDENS SKY POOL 3 Viaduct Gardens, Nine Elms, London, SW11 7AY **UNITED KINGDOM**

THE WORLD'S BEST SWIMMING POOLS

There is no pool in the world quite like the Embassy Gardens Sky Pool, located in London's Nine Elms neighborhood. Seemingly floating in the air, the transparent 25-meter pool connects two residential towers some 115 feet above the ground, creating a unique swimming experience for those without a fear of heights—and a unique view for passersby on the ground who can peer through the water to see the sky. Access to the pool is limited, however. Only members of the Embassy Gardens' Eg:le Club and their guests are able to swim here. You can take a peek at the listings, though, to see if there's a residence that intrigues you.

embassygardens.com/sky-pool

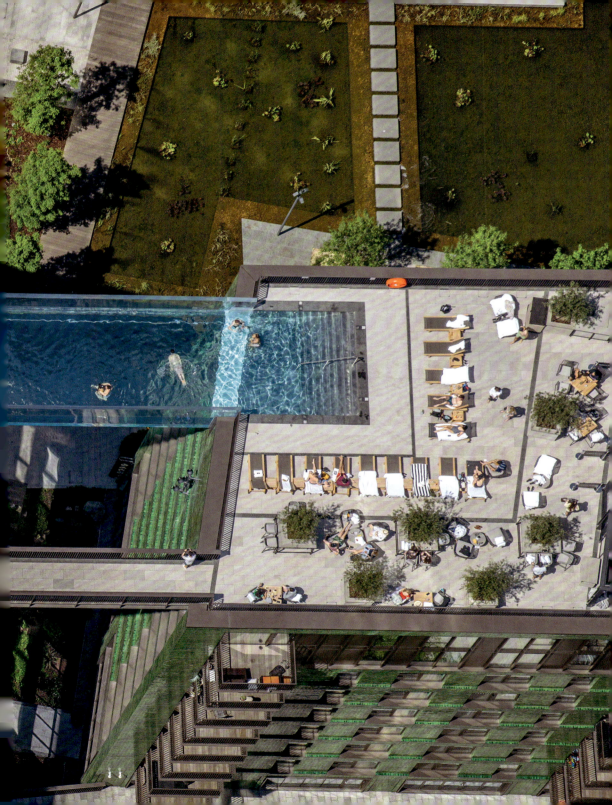

EUROPE

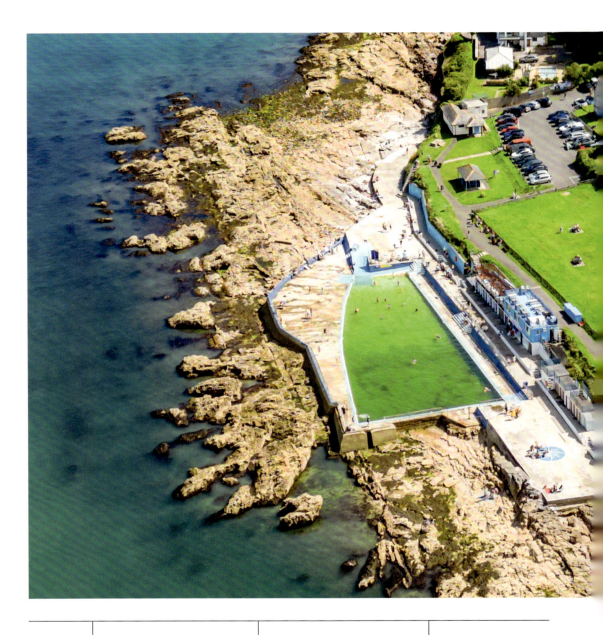

SHOALSTONE POOL Berry Head Road, Brixham, Devon, TQ5 9FT UNITED KINGDOM

THE WORLD'S BEST SWIMMING POOLS

Built on the site of a formal natural rock pool, Shoalstone Pool in Brixham opened to the public in 1896 as part of the great British lido tradition. The 53-meter pool fills with seawater during each high tide; its shallow end is ideal for children, while the deep end is prime for more serious swimming. The pool is open every summer, with a kiosk and café serving snacks poolside, and other vendors providing loungers and umbrellas. There's also an adjacent beach, where seasonal beach huts are available for rent.

EUROPE

The Fairy Pools on Scotland's Isle of Skye are a series of crystal-clear spring-fed pools connected by waterfalls, near the village of Carbost in Glenbrittle. Perhaps unsurprisingly, they're a favorite photo spot for visitors. Swimming is permitted here, but the pools are frigid, and it's advised you wear a wetsuit if you're taking a dip. While the Fairy Pools seem tranquil enough today, they have a dark history. They were the site of the Battle of Coire na Creiche, fought between the MacLeods of Dunvegan and the MacDonalds of Sleat. The battle was so bloody, legend says the Fairy Pools turned red.

| | **FAIRY POOLS** | Glenbrittle, Isle of Skye, Scotland, IV47 8TA | **UNITED KINGDOM** |

THE WORLD'S BEST SWIMMING POOLS

dunvegancastle.com/fairy-pools

NORTH & MIDDLE AMERICA

Cap Juluca is defined by its Morocco-meets-Santorini architecture: whitewashed structures with domes and arches dominate the palm-fringed landscape along Anguilla's best beach. They're complemented by azure water features throughout—most, if not all, of which are swimmable. There are pools everywhere: an infinity pool near the beach, private pools in the pool villas, and a pool in the spa. And, of course, there's that stunning beach, where you can trade swimming for water sports. It's no wonder this hotel has been a celebrity hot spot since it opened in 1988, and it continues to draw in new loyalists.

| | **CAP JULUCA, A BELMOND HOTEL** | Maundays Bay, A1-2640 | ANGUILLA |

THE WORLD'S BEST SWIMMING POOLS

belmond.com/hotels/north-america/caribbean/anguilla/belmond-cap-juluca

NORTH & MIDDLE AMERICA

CONCHI NATURAL POOL | Arikok National Park | ARUBA

THE WORLD'S BEST SWIMMING POOLS

Journey deep into Aruba's Arikok National Park, which comprises some 20 percent of the island, to find this not-so-secret but difficult-to-reach pair of rock pools. It'll take just shy of an hour to get there from the main entrance, and you'll need a 4×4 vehicle to make the trek. But your hard work will be well rewarded—the calm main natural pool is a delightful swimming hole, ringed by volcanic rock into which waves crash and douse the air with mist. There's also a much smaller natural pool tucked into the rocks above the main one for dipping.

aruba.com/us/explore/natural-pool

NORTH & MIDDLE AMERICA

 | **THE BATHS** | The Baths National Park, Virgin Gorda | **BRITISH VIRGIN ISLANDS**

At less than seven acres in size, The Baths is a little national park. But there is a lot packed into that space: namely, beautiful tidal pools tucked into giant granite boulders on the beach. This is one of the British Virgin Islands' most famous attractions, drawing in island-based day-trippers and cruise ship visitors en masse—go early or late in the day to avoid the crowds. In any case, it's well worth a visit to explore the calm blue waters shielded by the massive boulders.

NORTH & MIDDLE AMERICA

It's all about adventure at Pacuare Lodge, a luxury eco hotel deep in the rainforest of Costa Rica along the Pacuare River, and it begins even before you arrive. Most guests get to the property via whitewater raft, a very atypical transfer. Being that the river is an integral part of the property and its activities for guests, it should come as no surprise that Pacuare Lodge's elongated swimming pool overlooks its rushing waters—and the rainforest on its banks. It's the perfect spot to relax after a zip-lining excursion, a guided hike, or a visit to the indigenous Cabécar community.

PACUARE LODGE | Pacuare Reserve, Limón Province | COSTA RICA

THE WORLD'S BEST SWIMMING POOLS

NORTH & MIDDLE AMERICA

| **NAYARA TENTED CAMP** | Arenal Volcano National Park, La Fortuna, Alajuela Province | COSTA RICA |

In the shadow of Arenal Volcano, the sensational Nayara Tented Camp is all about eco glamour. It's part of the Nayara eco resort, which also includes Nayara Gardens and Nayara Springs. But at Nayara Tented Camp in particular, it's all about the sloths—the resort reforested part of its grounds to provide more natural habitat for sloths. It makes for some pretty spectacular landscaping, too. So as you're sitting in one of the hot spring-fed terraced pools or the private pool in your tented suite, look out at Arenal's smoking summit, and don't be surprised if a sloth is hanging out nearby.

NORTH & MIDDLE AMERICA

VILLA AVELLANA Prieta Estates, Peninsula Papagayo, Guanacaste COSTA RICA

THE WORLD'S BEST SWIMMING POOLS

At Villa Avellana, it's not only the pool that's breathtaking, but also the structure surrounding it. The villa is a private vacation rental in the exclusive Prieta Estates in Costa Rica's Peninsula Papagayo, offering an extraordinary 33,000 square feet of space for up to 23 guests in 10 rooms—it's essentially a private boutique hotel with a full staff. The main entertaining area is an indoor–outdoor complex that includes a 25-meter infinity lap pool, a lounge, and a bar. The house itself is tucked into the forest, but just beyond the trees you can see (and hear) the ocean.

NORTH & MIDDLE AMERICA

| | **UUNARTOQ HOT SPRING** | Uunartoq Island (uninhabited), between Qaqortoq and Nanortalik | **GREENLAND** |

THE WORLD'S BEST SWIMMING POOLS

Greenland may not be as geothermally active as nearby Iceland, but it does have its fair share of hot springs. The best one for soaking is on the uninhabited island of Uunartoq in South Greenland, where three springs feed a stone-dammed pool. The temperature is a balmy 100.4 degrees Fahrenheit, perfect for a relaxing soak as you watch massive icebergs float by. To get there, book a water taxi from Qaqortoq, the largest settlement in the region, which is about an hour away by boat. Since it is typically a little cold in Greenland, wear layers on the ride—there are changing facilities by the pool.

NORTH & MIDDLE AMERICA

| | **SILVERSANDS GRENADA** | Grand Anse Main Road, St. George | **GRENADA** |

THE WORLD'S BEST SWIMMING POOLS

At 100 meters long, Silversands Grenada's extraordinary swimming pool might just be the longest pool in the Caribbean. It stretches from the hotel all the way to the beach, lined with palm trees, loungers, and day beds along the way. If you'd prefer some privacy during your swim, book one of the eight private pool villas, each of which comes with a spacious main pool plus two heated plunge pools. You'll get much more than private pools, too—each of these residences has three or four bedrooms, a fully equipped kitchen, and a dedicated villa host.

silversandsgrenada.com/resorts/grand-anse

NORTH & MIDDLE AMERICA

| | **WALDORF ASTORIA LOS CABOS PEDREGAL** | Camino Del Mar 1, Cabo San Lucas, Baja California Sur, 23455 | MEXICO |

THE WORLD'S BEST SWIMMING POOLS

Your stay at the Waldorf Astoria Los Cabos Pedregal begins with a stroll through a 900-foot tunnel, out of which you emerge into what appears to be a luxe Mediterranean village. But this is Mexico, and that ocean you're gazing at is the Pacific. Along the beach is a gorgeous free-form pool that undulates like the waterline just beyond it—a thatched roof covers a swim-up bar right in its center. There's also a saltwater meditation pool for a more serene scene. Plus, every single accommodation, from standard rooms up to private homes, has a private plunge pool.

NORTH & MIDDLE AMERICA

CAREYES | Km 53.5, Carretera Melaque – Puerto Vallarta, Jalisco, 48894 | MEXICO

Italian banker Gian Franco Brignone is responsible for building this surreal arts and wellness paradise on Mexico's western shores, some three hours from Puerto Vallarta. Careyes is a 36,000-acre resort unlike any other in the country, filled with architectural wonders and art installations—but only on about three percent of the grounds. The rest remains a protected biosphere. But Careyes makes excellent use of its developed areas, perhaps none more so than its twin Ocean Castles, Sol de Oriente and Sol de Occidente. These marvelous structures, designed by French architect Jean-Claude Galibert, are private hilltop residences surrounded by perfectly circular infinity pools.

NORTH & MIDDLE AMERICA

| | **LAS VENTANAS AL PARAÍSO, A ROSEWOOD RESORT** | Km 19.5, Carretera Transpeninsular, San José del Cabo, Baja California Sur, 23405 | MEXICO |

THE WORLD'S BEST SWIMMING POOLS

It's hard to be far from a pool on the property of Las Ventanas al Paraíso in Los Cabos. There are eight of them at the Mediterranean-inspired resort, some expansive ones that practically appear to be an extension of the sea, while others are more intimate, tranquil spots. One of the highlights, though, is the 5,000-square-foot Oasis Pool, which is complemented by a lazy river with a grotto-like tunnel and waterfalls. No matter which pool you visit, there will always be a staffer on hand to provide drinks, fresh towels, or a cool spritz of evian spray.

rosewoodhotels.com/en/las-ventanas-los-cabos

NORTH & MIDDLE AMERICA

Is it strange to compare a beachy boutique hotel in Mexico to Venice? Perhaps. But I think it's apt, despite the differences in architecture. Just as the canals connect all parts of the city in Venice, a pool connects all parts of Punta Caliza on Isla Holbox. The hotel's multiple buildings feature white walls accented by red cedar wood, with towering palapa-style straw roofs—these earthy materials contrast well with the blue water in the pools. Each of the 14 rooms has its own pool but is also connected to the main pool, so you could swim anywhere if you wanted to.

PUNTA CALIZA	Paseo Kuka s/n Esquina Robalo, Isla Holbox, Quintana Roo, 77310	MEXICO

THE WORLD'S BEST SWIMMING POOLS

313   puntacaliza.com

THE WORLD'S BEST SWIMMING POOLS

NORTH & MIDDLE AMERICA

 | **CASA O'TE MITI** | Teitiare Estate, Calle Norte 200, Camino a Playa Escondida Sayulita, Nayarit, 63732 | MEXICO

THE WORLD'S BEST SWIMMING POOLS

This pretty six-room private vacation home in Sayulita, Mexico, is packed with hues that pop against the natural materials found throughout the property. By the ocean-view infinity pool, bubblegum pink is the accent color of choice, paired with a tiki bar filled with driftwood furnishings, vintage wood surfboards, and a thatched palapa roof. The house is located on a rocky point on the Teitiare Estate, a "pueblito" with various accommodations. Casa O'te Miti has a full staff, including a butler and a private chef.

teitiare.com/casa-ote-miti

NORTH & MIDDLE AMERICA

 | **CASA INSPIRACIÓN** | Calle Delfines s/n, Fraccionamiento Las Mantas, Puerto Escondido, Oaxaca, 70934 | MEXICO

THE WORLD'S BEST SWIMMING POOLS

Smooth river stones frame the cerulean pool at the six-bedroom Casa Inspiración, a paradisiacal private vacation home some 10 miles outside of the surfing capital Puerto Escondido on Mexico's Pacific coast. At the pool, however, it's not about the excitement of swell. The glass-like surface of the water pulls you in for more relaxing pursuits, like cooling off on a hot afternoon. Though at 20 meters in length, it is a good spot for swimming laps if you're feeling a bit more active. You can also visit the beach just in front of the casa if you're craving the action of the sea.

NORTH & MIDDLE AMERICA

CENOTE XCANAHALTUN | Temozón, Yucatán, 97744 | MEXICO

THE WORLD'S BEST SWIMMING POOLS

Across Mexico's Yucatán Peninsula are thousands of cenotes, or water-filled sinkholes, that formed when limestone caves collapsed. These natural pools are popular swimming holes, especially among visitors to the region, and as such, many of the more popular cenotes can become a little too crowded for a pleasurable experience. Not so for Cenote Xcanahaltun (yet). Located a half hour or so outside of the city of Valladolid, itself halfway between Cancún and Mérida, this cenote is still very cave-like rather than open to the sky, with a small natural skylight illuminating a stalactite-laden subterranean chamber filled with turquoise water.

NORTH & MIDDLE AMERICA

HIERVE EL AGUA | San Lorenzo Albarradas, Oaxaca, 70477 | MEXICO

You might've heard about petrified wood, but what about petrified waterfalls? You'll find one in the Mexican state of Oaxaca, about 90 minutes outside the city of Oaxaca. Waters emanating from a spring have trickled over a cliff, depositing minerals over thousands of years. The result is what looks like a static waterfall—this is Hierve el Agua. At the top are shallow natural pools of this mineral-rich spring water, as well as a few artificial pools that you can swim in. Before you cool off in the spring water, consider hiking down to the base of the waterfall to experience the optical illusion.

NORTH & MIDDLE AMERICA

You might expect most of Cabo's top resorts to be on the beach, and many certainly are. But Acre Resort bucks the trend—it's located inland in forested hills. That's why most of the accommodations are eco-chic tree houses, with a few stand-alone villas, too. Many guests know of Acre for its standout farm-to-table restaurant and bar, but it's becoming a wellness destination too, given its spa and free yoga classes. And then there's the matter of the postcard-perfect pool with an adjacent pool bar, surrounded by plenty of greenery. It's an ideal jungle retreat, which is far different from most of the resorts you'll find in the area.

| **ACRE RESORT CABO** | Calle Rincón de las Animas s/n, Animas Bajas, San José del Cabo, Baja California Sur, 23407 | MEXICO |

THE WORLD'S BEST SWIMMING POOLS

325   acreresort.com

NORTH & MIDDLE AMERICA

DORADO BEACH, A RITZ-CARLTON RESERVE | 100 Dorado Beach Drive, Dorado, 00646 | PUERTO RICO

THE WORLD'S BEST SWIMMING POOLS

What was once a pineapple, grapefruit, and coconut plantation in Puerto Rico has been transformed into the elegant Dorado resort, which includes Dorado Beach, a Ritz-Carlton Reserve. The original resort was opened in 1958 by Laurance S. Rockefeller, son of John D. Rockefeller, and it drew in high-profile clientele, from baseball stars Joe DiMaggio and Mickey Mantle, to Hollywood actors Elizabeth Taylor and Joan Crawford, to presidents John F. Kennedy and Dwight Eisenhower. Even if you're not an A-lister yourself, you can book a room here and enjoy the property's tropical-style pools fronting the beach.

ritzcarlton.com/en/hotels/sjudo-dorado-beach-a-ritz-carlton-reserve/overview

NORTH & MIDDLE AMERICA

| **BELLE MONT FARM** | The Village Kittitian Hill, St. Kitts | **SAINT KITTS AND NEVIS** |

THE WORLD'S BEST SWIMMING POOLS

Former sugar plantation Kittitian Hill is now home to Belle Mont Farm, one of the rare Caribbean retreats that has nothing to do with the beach. Instead, the focus is on the land—particularly organic and sustainable agricultural practices best represented by the restaurants here, which all incorporate local ingredients into their menus. The Great House, which has a replica sugar mill, is where you'll find the communal infinity pool, but many of the cottages, as well as the private villas, have their own plunge pools, too.

bellemontfarm.com

NORTH & MIDDLE AMERICA

Jade Mountain could very well be the most romantic honeymoon resort in the Caribbean. That's because 24 of its sprawling open-air suites, which the hotel refers to as "sanctuaries," are exceptionally private. You could choose to remain in your suite your entire stay—butlers are on hand to serve you meals, while you can spend your days swimming in the massive infinity pools (they're 400 to 900 square feet) and taking in the jaw-dropping views of the Pitons from your prime mountainside location. There are also five whirlpool suites without pools, but I think the pools are worth the splurge.

JADE MOUNTAIN RESORT | 100 Anse Chastanet Road, Soufrière | ST. LUCIA

THE WORLD'S BEST SWIMMING POOLS

jademountain.com

NORTH & MIDDLE AMERICA

| | **MANDARIN ORIENTAL, CANOUAN** | Carenage Bay, Canouan Island, VC0450 | **SAINT VINCENT AND THE GRENADINES** |

THE WORLD'S BEST SWIMMING POOLS

Canouan is still something of a well-kept secret—it's a tiny Caribbean island in the Grenadines, one that's been referred to as the place "billionaires go to escape millionaires." Of course, you don't really have to be a billionaire to stay here, though it certainly helps to be well-heeled to splurge on a multi-bedroom villa with a private pool at the Mandarin Oriental, Canouan. The beachfront luxury resort does have a shared infinity pool that's worth a swim, though, lined with hot-pink umbrellas and offering a perfect view of the sea.

NORTH & MIDDLE AMERICA

WYMARA TURKS AND CAICOS

218 Lower Bight Road, Grace Bay, Providenciales, TKCA 1ZZ

TURKS AND CAICOS

THE WORLD'S BEST SWIMMING POOLS

What impresses me most about Wymara's swimming pools is their variety—it's not all about your run-of-the-mill oceanfront infinity pools here. The main pool is an impressive 7,000-square-foot spot with cabanas set on islands in the middle of it, while the spa pool is a 25-meter lap pool in a grassy courtyard. And many of the architecturally intriguing villas have private plunge pools, some of which are built into rocky outcrops. But the best pool, in my opinion, is the ocean pool, inspired by Australia's famous rock pools. It's a calm spot protected from swells and currents, but otherwise part of the ocean.

NORTH & MIDDLE AMERICA

SHERATON WAIKIKI | 2255 Kalākaua Avenue, Honolulu, Hawaii 96815 | UNITED STATES

Sheraton Waikiki is a stalwart in the Honolulu hotel scene, and its pools are one of many reasons why travelers return to the property year after year. There are two, and they cater to very different audiences. The first is the lagoon-like Helumoa Playground Pool, designed with families in mind. It's technically two pools separated by a small waterslide, with a larger waterslide tucked into the rocks. There are also whirlpool spas and semi-submerged sunning benches to appeal to adults. The second pool is the adults-only Edge Infinity Pool, which has a 130-foot-long edge that seemingly meets the sea. By night, it turns into a vibrant lounge scene.

NORTH & MIDDLE AMERICA

THE SAGAMORE RESORT | 110 Sagamore Road, Bolton Landing, New York 12814 | UNITED STATES

THE WORLD'S BEST SWIMMING POOLS

The Sagamore Resort is one of the great Adirondack resorts of a bygone era, built in 1883 on a private island in Upstate New York's Lake George. The region is known as the birthplace of the American vacation—the term is derived from the fact that East Coast city dwellers "vacated" their homes for the summer for a respite in nature. And at The Sagamore, you can still experience that old-school grandeur. I'm particularly impressed by the pool here, which almost has a Lake Como flair between the verdant landscaping and the panoramic lake views.

NORTH & MIDDLE AMERICA

GINNIE SPRINGS 5000 NE 60th Avenue, High Springs, Florida 32643 UNITED STATES

The waters of Ginnie Springs are known for two things: their perfect 72-degree Fahrenheit temperature and their clarity. Regarding the latter, famed French oceanographer and filmmaker Jacques Cousteau wrote of the springs: "visibility forever." While you can certainly come here just for a swim or snorkel, Ginnie Springs is also known as a dive site, thanks to its underwater caves. You can rent equipment on site if you're certified, and there are also training programs available for newbies. Ginnie Springs is also a popular destination for paddling, whether via kayak or stand-up paddleboard.

NORTH & MIDDLE AMERICA

LOWER FALLS AT ROBERT H. TREMAN STATE PARK

105 Enfield Falls Road, Ithaca, New York 14850

UNITED STATES

THE WORLD'S BEST SWIMMING POOLS

New York's Robert H. Treman State Park in the Finger Lakes region has 12 waterfalls cascading through Enfield Glen—including the stunning 115-foot Lucifer Falls—which makes hiking an absolute delight here. If you're visiting in the summer, you'll probably want to go for a dip, which you can do in the large swimming area beneath the 40-foot-tall Lower Falls (and nowhere else—safety first!). It's a picturesque area with refreshingly cool waters, plus a diving platform for the brave, picnic tables, and barbecue grills.

NORTH & MIDDLE AMERICA

| | **GARDEN OF THE GODS RESORT & CLUB** | 3320 Mesa Road, Colorado Springs, Colorado 80904 | UNITED STATES |

Is it a conceit to name your resort Garden of the Gods? Maybe. But I think this particular property can boast that title, particularly regarding its view. It overlooks Colorado's famed Garden of the Gods, a National Natural Landmark, where dramatic red rocks jut out from a deep green forest. And at the resort, the adults-only infinity pool has the best vantage point. It's heated to 84 degrees Fahrenheit year-round, so you can enjoy the vistas no matter the season. For families, there are two other pool complexes: Three Graces Pool Complex, which has a bar and grill, and Recreation Center Pools, which has a kids' splash pad.

gardenofthegodsresort.com

NORTH & MIDDLE AMERICA

Big Sur's acclaimed Post Ranch Inn takes infinity pools to new heights—literally. Its three heated infinity pools sit atop a 1,200-foot cliff above the Pacific Ocean—the property is frequently in the clouds. The inn was originally the homestead of William B. Post, who claimed 160 acres in 1867, and his original cabin still stands on the property today. But in 1992, the Post Ranch Inn as we know it today welcomed its first guests, continuing to do so for the past few decades with wellness offerings, fine dining, and utter relaxation.

POST RANCH INN 47900 Highway 1, Big Sur, California 93920 UNITED STATES

THE WORLD'S BEST SWIMMING POOLS

NORTH & MIDDLE AMERICA

ENCHANTMENT RESORT

525 Boynton Canyon Road, Sedona, Arizona 86336

UNITED STATES

THE WORLD'S BEST SWIMMING POOLS

The backdrop to the Enchantment Resort is on another level: Boynton Canyon's walls comprising striated red rock are sandwiched between the blues of the sky and the resort's main pool (one of three). The resort is located some nine miles from downtown Sedona, but it feels as if it could be hundreds of miles away in the middle of the desert. Guests of this serene property also have access to the exclusive Mii Amo destination spa, which takes advantage of its location in what's considered to be one of Sedona's major energy vortexes.

NORTH & MIDDLE AMERICA

On the Havasupai Indian Reservation in Arizona are the iconic Havasu Falls, one of the most sought-after hiking destinations in the state. Permits to hike here (and camp overnight or book a room at the Havasupai Lodge) are extremely limited, but those who secure one are treated to this colorful waterfall, complete with geothermally heated waters that hover around 70 degrees Fahrenheit year-round. But Havasu Falls isn't the only cascade here—don't miss Navajo Falls, Beaver Falls, and Mooney Falls, too. The gentle pools of Beaver Falls are particularly excellent swimming spots.

| **HAVASU FALLS** | Havasupai Indian Reservation, Arizona | UNITED STATES |

NORTH & MIDDLE AMERICA

BEVERLY HILLS HOTEL 9641 Sunset Boulevard, Beverly Hills, California 90210 UNITED STATES

THE WORLD'S BEST SWIMMING POOLS

Los Angeles and swimming pools go hand in hand. But of the many spots to take a dip, perhaps none is so famous as the pool at the iconic Beverly Hills Hotel. The hotel opened in 1912—two years before Beverly Hills was incorporated as a city—and has since entertained all manner of celebrities through its years, many of whom lounged poolside or even went for a swim. (Katharine Hepburn, for example, was reportedly a fan of diving in after playing tennis.) Tall palms serve as a backdrop here, with cabanas in the hotel's signature pink lining the bright-blue water.

dorchestercollection.com/los-angeles/the-beverly-hills-hotel

NORTH & MIDDLE AMERICA

BARTON SPRINGS POOL

2131 William Barton Drive,
Austin, Texas 78746

UNITED STATES

THE WORLD'S BEST SWIMMING POOLS

Austin might be a fairly built-up city, but there's plenty of green space to be found. In particular, there's the 358-acre Zilker Park, where you'll find the famous Barton Springs Pool, a favorite spot for locals to cool down in the summer. The three-acre pool is fed by natural springs, and its waters, which are as deep as 18 feet in some spots, remain a refreshing 68–70 degrees Fahrenheit at all times. Beyond being one of the best swimming pools in Austin (and certainly the best natural one), it has another claim to fame: actor and filmmaker Robert Redford learned to swim here as a child.

austintexas.gov/department/barton-springs-pool

NORTH & MIDDLE AMERICA

| | **FOUR SEASONS HUALALAI** | 72-100 Ka'ūpūlehu Drive, Kailua-Kona, Hawaii 96740 | **UNITED STATES** |

Located on Hawaii's Big Island, the Four Seasons Hualalai comprises 865 oceanfront acres some 15 miles down the road from Kailua-Kona. Spread throughout are multiple pools, from the infinity-edge Sea Shell Pool, which is a more traditional resort pool, to King's Pond, a special saltwater aquarium pool carved into lava rock and filled with marine life, including the resort's resident eagle ray, Kainalu. In the latter, marine biologists are on hand for educational programming to enhance your swimming experience. For guests seeking a private swim, book one of the villas, each of which has a pool.

NORTH & MIDDLE AMERICA

TRAVERTINE HOT SPRINGS | Bridgeport, California 93517 | UNITED STATES

THE WORLD'S BEST SWIMMING POOLS

Located near the town of Bridgeport along the California–Nevada border, the Travertine Hot Springs look like an alien landscape—sculptural travertine terraces hold around a half dozen or so geothermally heated soaking pools. The travertine comes from the calcium carbonate in the mineral water, which is deposited over time in the desert landscape. As you're enjoying the hot tub–like pools, you can gaze out to the snow-capped mountains beyond. It's a serene experience if you have the pools to yourself, though don't be surprised if there are others around. These hot springs are not a well-kept secret!

NORTH & MIDDLE AMERICA

Yes, it seems a bit surprising that an airport hotel has one of the best swimming pools in the world. But the TWA Hotel at New York's John F. Kennedy International Airport is a special spot. Housed in the Eero Saarinen–designed former TWA terminal, the hotel has a distinct mid-century flair and a focus on aviation history that both architecture buffs and avgeeks will enjoy. Guests of the hotel—and that includes those who book a day rate on a layover—are welcome to use the rooftop infinity pool, which overlooks one of JFK's runways. It's open year-round and heated to a balmy 95 degrees Fahrenheit in the winter.

TWA HOTEL

One Idlewild Drive, Jamaica, Queens, New York, New York 11430

UNITED STATES

THE WORLD'S BEST SWIMMING POOLS

363   twahotel.com

NORTH & MIDDLE AMERICA

| | **CASTLE HOT SPRINGS** | 5050 N. Castle Hot Springs Road, Morristown, Arizona 85342 | UNITED STATES |

Long before it was established as Arizona's first wellness retreat in 1896, Castle Hot Springs (or, more specifically, its mineral waters) was used by the indigenous Yavapai for a healing soak. Then came the travelers from afar, including some of America's most prominent 20th-century families, such as the Rockefellers, the Vanderbilts, and the Astors. Its next phase of life was a recovery retreat for World War II soldiers— John F. Kennedy spent time here—before returning to a leisure resort and eventually falling derelict. Today, Castle Hot Springs has been revitalized, and guests once again come to soak in the mineral waters.

NORTH & MIDDLE AMERICA

HAMILTON POOL PRESERVE   24300 Hamilton Road, Dripping Springs, Texas 78620   UNITED STATES

In Texas Hill Country some 30 miles outside of Austin, you'll find the Hamilton Pool Preserve, a natural swimming hole designated a preserve in 1990. The pool isn't just a simple body of water, though. Here, a waterfall flows over a cave-like rocky overhang into emerald waters below, creating a stunning scene. To get to the Hamilton Pool Preserve, you'll have to hike a rocky quarter-mile trail both out and back, so bring reasonable footwear. Also, be aware that the pool can be closed due to certain conditions like bacterial growth or heavy rains—check with Travis County ahead of your visit.

parks.traviscountytx.gov/parks/hamilton-pool-preserve

NORTH & MIDDLE AMERICA

MIRADA LAGOON | 31461 Mirada Boulevard, San Antonio, Florida 33576 | UNITED STATES

THE WORLD'S BEST SWIMMING POOLS

Sure, Florida may have more than 1,000 miles of coastline, but many inland areas don't have convenient access to vast bodies of water. That's not the case in the community of San Antonio. It's home to Mirada, the largest man-made lagoon in the U.S., which has a surface area of some 15 acres. It's a resort-like paradise for those who can't make it to the beach, with a large floating obstacle course on the water, a swim-up bar for adults, and even sandy mini-islands for sunning. In fact, it's not the only such lagoon in Florida—the company MetroLagoons is building a veritable empire of man-made lagoons in the state, a handful of which are already finished.

NORTH & MIDDLE AMERICA

| THREE SISTERS SPRINGS | 917 Three Sisters Springs Trail, Crystal River, Florida 34429 | UNITED STATES |

THE WORLD'S BEST SWIMMING POOLS

Part of the Crystal River National Wildlife Refuge on Florida's Gulf Coast, the Three Sisters Springs are known as the winter home of manatees, who swim here from the Gulf of Mexico to enjoy the warm geothermal waters. You, too, can enjoy the waters by kayaking in, donning a snorkel mask, and jumping in. The manatees are usually in residence only during the cold winter months, but the springs are swimmable year-round and worth a visit no matter the season. Note that you can't enter the water from the land surrounding the springs—you have to enter via the waterways to prevent land erosion. (Hence those kayaks!)

threesistersspringsvisitor.org/sisters

NORTH & MIDDLE AMERICA

HOTEL FIGUEROA

939 S. Figueroa Street, Los Angeles, California 90015

UNITED STATES

THE WORLD'S BEST SWIMMING POOLS

The Spanish Colonial-style Hotel Figueroa in Downtown L.A. opened in 1926 as a women's business hotel, and it remains a vibrant part of the neighborhood social scene today, not only for its various restaurants and bars, but also for its pool. Now, said pool has a rather intriguing shape—it resembles a coffin—but the lushly gardened pool deck is a rather lively spot. If you're not a guest, you can book a day pass to swim here; it comes with perks like free Wi-Fi, a free smoothie, and discounted parking, too.

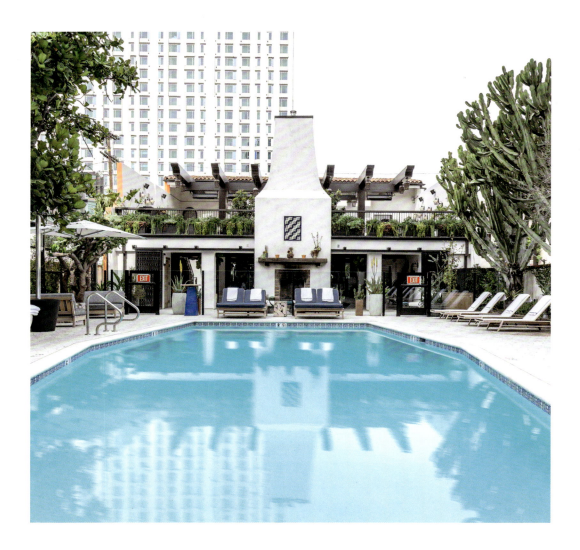

hotelfigueroa.com

| | **VIKING OCTANTIS AND VIKING POLARIS** | N/A | N/A |

THE WORLD'S BEST SWIMMING POOLS

Twin sisters Viking Octantis and Viking Polaris might be expedition cruise ships capable of sailing into the frigid polar regions, but inside, they're extraordinarily cozy and plush. While older expedition ships might not have very many luxury amenities, these two certainly do. The spa, for example, is one of the most beautiful spots on the ship. Here you'll find a spacious indoor swimming pool next to floor-to-ceiling windows—it's surreal to see giant icebergs floating by while you're reclining on a heated lounger. Beyond the pool, there's a full thermal circuit here, with one of my personal favorite stations being the badestamp, a Nordic-style hot tub in an open-air room.

OCEANIA

MONA VALE ROCKPOOL   1 Surfview Road, Mona Vale, New South Wales, 2103   AUSTRALIA

THE WORLD'S BEST SWIMMING POOLS

Located on the rocky tip of a sandspit, Mona Vale Rockpool in the northern Sydney suburb of Mona Vale was once a natural rock pool. But in the 1930s, the pool was enlarged to its current 30-meter span, and today, there's also a smaller, shallower pool for children. When the tide is in, the rocks surrounding the pool are covered by the sea, creating the illusion that the pool is floating among the waves. Keep an eye out for wildlife as you swim your laps—some swimmers have seen dolphins around the pool.

northernbeaches.nsw.gov.au/things-to-do/recreation-area/mona-vale-rockpool

OCEANIA

| | **BRONTE BATHS** | Beach Park, Bronte Road, Bronte, New South Wales, 2024 | AUSTRALIA |

THE WORLD'S BEST SWIMMING POOLS

In the mid- to late 19th century, this swimming spot embedded in the sandstone cliffs south of Sydney's famous Bondi Beach was known as "the bogey hole at South Nelson Bay." But in 1883, the local council set aside some budget to build a more formal pool here called the Bronte Baths, named for the neighboring beach, which is still enjoyed by swimmers today. If the chilly waters aren't for you, you can still get a beautiful view of the pools from the Bronte Baths Viewpoint above it. While this pool might be a touch less famous than the Bondi Baths and their famous Bondi Icebergs swimming club, it's a fabulous free alternative.

OCEANIA

DAWN FRASER BATHS | Elkington Park, Fitzroy Avenue, Balmain, Sydney, New South Wales, 2041 | AUSTRALIA

Built in the 1880s, Dawn Fraser Baths in Sydney is the oldest existing swimming pool in Australia, and it's also home to the country's oldest swimming club. Its name, however, dates back to the 1960s—it's named for the Australian swimming champion and Olympic gold medalist Dawn Fraser, who learned to swim here. Surrounded by wooden platforms frequently lined with sunbathers, the pool is divided into sections for lap swimming and casual swimming. Because this is a tidal pool, you can swim here only when the tides (and other water conditions) allow, so make sure you call ahead to find out its status.

OCEANIA

The Ross Jones Memorial Pool off Coogee Beach was named in honor of a local alderman, who held his position from 1934 to 1937 and was affiliated with the neighboring Coogee Surf Life Saving Club. It was built in 1947 and remains popular today, not only for its calm waters in an otherwise choppy spot, but also for its sandcastle-like concrete crenellations that separate it from the sea. As such, it's a favorite spot for both swimmers and photographers alike. There are two pools, a larger one and a smaller one, and the latter is best for children. That said, sometimes it's devoid of water and functions more as a sandbox instead—appropriate for the architecture of the pool.

ROSS JONES MEMORIAL ROCKPOOL | 133R Beach Street, Coogee, New South Wales, 2034 | AUSTRALIA

THE WORLD'S BEST SWIMMING POOLS

randwick.nsw.gov.au/facilities-and-recreation/beaches-and-coast/ocean-pools

OCEANIA

| CARDWELL SPA POOL | Brasenose Street/Cardwell Forest Drive, Cardwell, Cassowary Coast Region, Queensland, 4849 | AUSTRALIA |

THE WORLD'S BEST SWIMMING POOLS

It's all about contrast at Cardwell Spa Pool—contrasting colors, that is. The pool, which is part of a spring-fed seasonal creek near the town of Cardwell, some 2.5 hours from Cairns, has milky-blue waters that stand out among the bright-green eucalyptus trees surrounding it. That color, according to geologists, comes from the water's mineral content. It's best to visit the Cardwell Spa Pool between May and September, which is the area's dry season. During the wet season, rains can flush the creek out, changing its bright-blue hue.

OCEANIA

Bogey Hole might look as if it's naturally occurring, but it was, in fact, hand-hewn by convicts in 1819 for James Thomas Morisset, the Commandant of Newcastle. It's one of the earliest known purpose-built swimming pools in Australia, though it actually might be an enlargement of a natural swimming hole that existed before the pool's construction. On a calm day, the pool might seem quite placid, but beware—waves are known to crash over the pool's stone wall, seemingly out of nowhere. Keep your belongings well away from the edge!

BOGEY HOLE

Shortland Esplanade, Newcastle, New South Wales, 2300

AUSTRALIA

THE WORLD'S BEST SWIMMING POOLS

387 visitnsw.com/destinations/north-coast/newcastle-area/newcastle/attractions/bogey-hole

OCEANIA

 | **NUKUTEPIPI PRIVATE ISLAND** | — | FRENCH POLYNESIA

If it's exclusivity you seek during your swim, you'll undoubtedly find it at Nukutepipi Private Island, a small atoll in French Polynesia's Tuamotus owned by Cirque du Soleil co-founder Guy Laliberté. The island can accommodate up to 52 guests across its slew of bills and bungalows, but it's an exclusive-use property, so the only people who will be there are the guests you invite (and the staff, of course). Built into a sand-toned platform, the main pool almost appears as if it's hovering over the beach, and it's a delightful spot to take a dip on a hot afternoon.

OCEANIA

| | **FOUR SEASONS RESORT BORA BORA** | Motu Tehotu, BP 547, Bora Bora, 98730 | **FRENCH POLYNESIA** |

THE WORLD'S BEST SWIMMING POOLS

When you imagine a perfect tropical pool at a beachside resort, you're probably picturing something like the one you'll find at the Four Seasons Resort Bora Bora. The large free-form pool appears to meander between palm trees, curving around a row of elegant thatched-roof cabanas. In the distance is the bright-blue sea, which might just tempt you to leave the pool for the beach. But there's no doubt you'll return—unless you book an overwater bungalow with a private plunge pool or a multi-bedroom villa with a private infinity pool. Those might override the main pool!

fourseasons.com/borabora

OCEANIA

**ST. REGIS
BORA BORA** Motu Ome'e, BP 506,
Bora Bora, 98730 FRENCH
POLYNESIA

In my humble opinion, you can't go wrong with any of the three communal pools at St. Regis Bora Bora. At the main pool, a swim-up bar allows you to order cocktails from Aparima Bar without ever leaving the water. Or you could reserve a cabana at the adults-only Oasis Pool, which is perfect for a lovely little pool date. But my personal favorite pool is the Lagoonarium, a massive saltwater lagoon filled with colorful fish that's perfect for snorkeling. From here, you'll also get a perfect view of Bora Bora's iconic Mount Otemanu.

marriott.com/en-us/hotels/bobxr-the-st-regis-bora-bora-resort/overview

OCEANIA

The French overseas territory of New Caledonia is perhaps not one of the most well-known destinations in the world. But if you visit this remarkable archipelago in Melanesia, you'll be treated to some pretty spectacular swimming spots, including Piscine Naturelle d'Oro on the Isle of Pines. Protected from the ocean by a rock barrier, this lagoon serves as something of a natural aquarium—yes, you can snorkel here! What makes this pool stand out is its fringe of pine trees, which are not necessarily something you'd expect in a tropical setting. And that's why this island is named for its trees!

| **PISCINE NATURELLE D'ORO** | Yuate Tremwatre, Isle of Pines | **NEW CALEDONIA** |

OCEANIA

| | **HUKA LODGE** | 271 Huka Falls Road, Wairakei, Taupo, 3384 | NEW ZEALAND |

One of the most exclusive accommodations in New Zealand, Huka Lodge on the Waikato River near Lake Taupo was once a humble fisherman's camp. Now, a century later, it's a 17-acre luxury resort with 20 suites and two cottages—and amenities like a spa, a croquet lawn, and tennis and pétanque courts, not to mention exquisite culinary experiences that focus on local ingredients. After a long day fly-fishing or mountain biking, guests can soak in a heated outdoor pool or one of the two spa pools for a little relaxation. It's an absolutely distinguished retreat that epitomizes an elegant country getaway.

OCEANIA

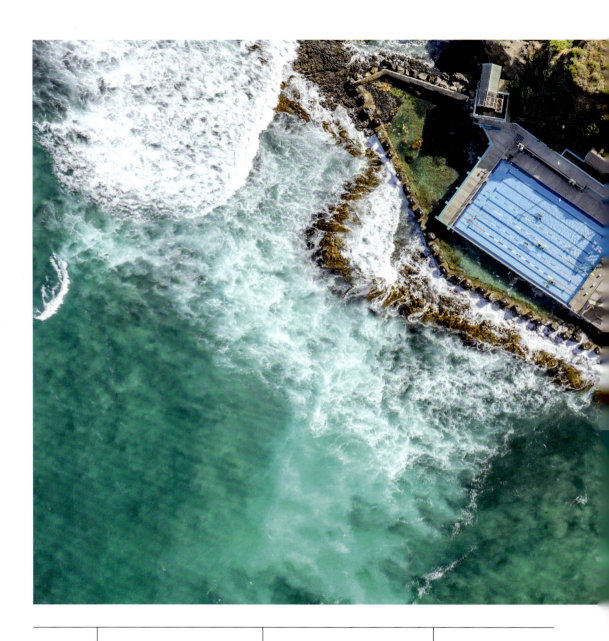

| | ST. CLAIR HOT SALT WATER POOL | Esplanade, St. Clair, Dunedin, 9012 | NEW ZEALAND |

THE WORLD'S BEST SWIMMING POOLS

The ocean in Dunedin is notoriously chilly, but thanks to the St. Clair Hot Salt Water Pool, you can enjoy the sea at a much more comfortable temperature: 82.4 degrees Fahrenheit, to be precise. The pool was originally built in the late 19th century and has since expanded to include a toddler pool, changing facilities, and a year-round café. But the star remains the 25-meter main pool, which has six lanes for lap swims. You can purchase a day pass to get in, but it's worth noting that guests of the nearby Hotel St. Clair receive complimentary access to the pool during their stay.

dunedin.govt.nz/community-facilities/swimming-pools/st-clair-pool

OCEANIA

When you book a stay at Aro Ha Wellness Retreat, you're not visiting for pure relaxation. You're here to totally recalibrate your body and mind, and that means you'll be putting in some work. Fortunately, part of the wellness prescription includes "contrast therapy," or, in other words, a thermal circuit at the spa. The outdoor plunge pools are particularly noteworthy for their exceptional views—the retreat is located in New Zealand's picturesque Southern Alps, a region that's a frequent favorite of filmmakers as an otherworldly setting. You'll also be treated to a daily massage to soothe your aching muscles after long hikes and fitness classes.

ARO HA WELLNESS RETREAT

33 Station Valley Road, Glenorchy, 9350

NEW ZEALAND

THE WORLD'S BEST SWIMMING POOLS

aro-ha.com

OCEANIA

TO-SUA OCEAN TRENCH | Lotofaga, Upolu | SAMOA

THE WORLD'S BEST SWIMMING POOLS

If you're afraid of heights, this might not be the pool for you. But trust me, it's worth conquering that fear. To-Sua means "giant swimming hole," and it's an apt name for this spot—it's a 100-foot-deep volcanic cave that's collapsed into an ocean-fed natural pool. To get into its blue-green waters, you'll have to climb some 65 feet down a ladder, or make the plunge from To-Sua's edge, if you're particularly brave (or perhaps foolish). If the drop isn't calling to you, you can simply peek over the edge, then take your leave and head for the surrounding gardens or adjacent Fagaoneone Beach.

405 samoa.travel/plan-book/activities/to-sua-ocean-trench

OCEANIA

| | **NANDA BLUE HOLE** | East Coast Road, Natawa, Sanma Province | VANUATU |

THE WORLD'S BEST SWIMMING POOLS

Nanda Blue Hole is one of the many gorgeous natural freshwater pools on the island of Espiritu Santo in Vanuatu. It, along with its neighbors, formed when fresh water carved a hole into the limestone rock formed from ancient coral reefs. The result is a spectacularly blue pool that's perfect for cooling off on a hot day. Nanda Blue Hole, also known as Jackie's Blue Hole after the woman who owns the land on which it sits, has the added perks of an adjacent bar and picnic area for day-trippers.

SOUTH AMERICA

| **ENTRE CIELOS WINE & WELLNESS HOTEL** | Guardia Vieja 1998, Luján de Cuyo, Mendoza | ARGENTINA |

THE WORLD'S BEST SWIMMING POOLS

While most accommodations in Argentina's Mendoza wine region are of the more rustic aesthetic, Entre Cielos is decidedly not. The boutique hotel is all about contemporary design, from the colorful interiors of its 24 rooms to the stark-white decor around the pool. One could argue that the white umbrellas by the loungers mimic the snow-capped peaks of the Andes by design. The property is a working vineyard, so plan on drinking plenty of Malbec while you're here. And when you're not imbibing by the pool, you can head into the spa, where you'll find Latin America's first traditional hammam.

SOUTH AMERICA

FOUR SEASONS BUENOS AIRES | 1086/88 Posadas, Buenos Aires | ARGENTINA

At the Four Seasons Buenos Aires, it's not necessarily the pool itself that's the main attraction; it's what's behind it. The hotel is housed in an early 20th-century mansion—and an adjacent high-rise—but it's the former structure that provides the backdrop to the Roman-style pool (the only outdoor pool in the tony Recoleta neighborhood, I might add). The Belle Époque La Mansión, as it's called, is where you'll find seven extravagant suites done up in period style. If you choose a room in the tower, you'll find more modern furnishings, but they'll still have some French flair.

SOUTH AMERICA

LAGOONS AT LENÇÓIS MARANHENSES NATIONAL PARK | Lençóis Maranhenses National Park, Maranhão | BRAZIL

THE WORLD'S BEST SWIMMING POOLS

The ephemeral lagoons at Brazil's Lençóis Maranhenses National Park are a natural wonder. During the rainy season, which runs from January to June, the valleys between the towering white sand dunes fill with fresh water, creating pools of varying shades of blue. And yes, many of these lagoons are swimmable. Definitely hire a guide to take you around, as you'll need a four-wheel-drive vehicle to make it through the dunes—and someone who knows how to navigate the 600-square-mile park! Remember, the lagoons are seasonal, and they're usually dried up by October.

icmbio.gov.br/parnalencoismaranhenses/visitant-guide.html

SOUTH AMERICA

Formerly a Four Seasons, and now a JW Marriott, this property is located in São Paulo's Chácara Santo Antônio business district. The neighborhood might not have the cachet of nearby Jardins, but the hotel certainly does. It's filled not only with art—São Paulo is, after all, a hub for Brazil's creatives—but also with striking interior design. A standout is the red spiral staircase that is undoubtedly a focal point of the hotel, visible from the floating lobby bar. But the real treat, at least in my opinion, is the indoor–outdoor pool in the spa. Behind the outdoor portion is a fabulous green wall, while inside, you'll find bold marble as a backdrop.

	JW MARRIOTT HOTEL SÃO PAULO	Torre Hotel, Avenida Das Nações Unidas, 14401 - Chácara Santo Antônio, São Paulo, 04794-000	BRAZIL

THE WORLD'S BEST SWIMMING POOLS

415 marriott.com/en-us/hotels/saojw-jw-marriott-hotel-sao-paulo/overview

SOUTH AMERICA

| **HOTEL FASANO RIO DE JANEIRO** | Avenida Vieira Souto, 80, Ipanema, Rio de Janeiro, 22420-002 | BRAZIL |

THE WORLD'S BEST SWIMMING POOLS

Rio de Janeiro's beaches are among the most famous in the world, so it's no surprise that some visitors to the city might choose the sea over a pool. But the infinity pool at the Hotel Fasano Rio de Janeiro might be able to change their minds, thanks to its views over the beaches of Ipanema and Leblon, as well as the Two Brothers and Corcovado mountains. (Not to mention it's right on Ipanema Beach, so you can easily switch between the two.) The hotel is the first project in Brazil by iconic designer Philippe Starck, and he's brought to it his signature avant-garde style, though it's tempered beautifully by natural elements and serene moments—such as what you'll find at the pool.

SOUTH AMERICA

| | **SAN ALFONSO DEL MAR** | Algarrobo, Valparaíso | CHILE |

THE WORLD'S BEST SWIMMING POOLS

Can you imagine a pool large enough that you can sail boats on it? Well, you don't need to imagine it—it's real. The San Alfonso del Mar resort in Algarrobo, Chile, some 60 miles outside of Santiago, is home to one of the world's largest swimming pools, and it really is spectacularly massive. It has a surface area of 20 acres and a depth of 11.5 feet at its deepest, holding 66 million gallons of salt water. Interestingly, it's located right on the coast, but the water here is too rough for swimming or other water sports; hence the creation of the pool.

SOUTH AMERICA

| | **VIK CHILE** | Rincon de Millahue SN, San Vicente de Tagua Tagua, San Vicente, O'Higgins, 2970001 | CHILE |

THE WORLD'S BEST SWIMMING POOLS

Vik Chile is many things. It's an 11,000-acre nature reserve, a working vineyard, a spa, and a hotel, all set within the picturesque Millahue Valley, about a two-hour drive from Santiago. It could also be considered something of an art museum, with works by such notable artists as Anselm Kiefer and Roberto Matta. And among the many amenities, there is, indeed, an infinity-edge pool looking out across the valley. But the view behind the pool is impressive, too— the hotel has an undulating titanium-and-bronze roof that looks like a ribbon fluttering in the breeze.

vikwine.com/en/vik-hotel

SOUTH AMERICA

Patagonia has an awe-inspiring landscape all its own, and at Tierra Patagonia Hotel & Spa, you're right in the middle of it. More specifically, you're on the shore of Lake Sarmiento looking right at the granite peaks of Torres del Paine National Park, in a curved wooden building that's designed to blend in with the surroundings. After a long day of hiking around the park, come back to spend a few hours at the spa, where you'll find an indoor pool with floor-to-ceiling windows that let you enjoy the ever-changing light across the mountains. On occasion, guanacos (a cousin to llamas and alpacas) and rheas (a cousin to ostriches and emus) will meander past.

| | **TIERRA PATAGONIA HOTEL & SPA** | On the edge of Torres del Paine National Park | CHILE |

SOUTH AMERICA

| | **TIERRA ATACAMA HOTEL & SPA** | Calle Séquitor s/n, San Pedro de Atacama, Antofagasta, 1410000 | CHILE |

THE WORLD'S BEST SWIMMING POOLS

At Tierra Atacama, the spa is called Uma, which means "water" in the Aymara language. Appropriately, water plays a big role here, from the steam room and indoor pool to the outdoor hot tub and infinity pool. In the latter two, you'll be soaking in a desert garden with views of the Licancabur volcano, which sometimes graces onlookers with a smoky show. The lodge itself is ideally located for numerous desert adventures, from hiking through canyons and up volcanoes to swimming in the salty Cejar lagoon on the salt flats. And, of course, there's always stargazing—this is one of the best places to look at the night sky.

SOUTH AMERICA

WARA HOTEL | La Cristiana s/n, Sector Cerro Negro Chamonate, Copiapó, 1530000 | CHILE

THE WORLD'S BEST SWIMMING POOLS

The pool at the Wara Hotel in the Atacama Desert might not be the largest or the flashiest, but it has heart, and that's just as important as a superlative. The pool is part of the central hub of the boutique seven-room property, and it exudes a desert-chic rusticity with thatched umbrellas and cacti. Though it may be small, the Wara Hotel has hosted some A-list guests. The cast of the 2015 film *The 33* about the 2010 Copiapó mining accident—including Antonio Banderas, Juliette Binoche, and Gabriel Byrne—stayed here during production. Each of the seven rooms has a private garden, an en suite bath with a soaking tub, and a fireplace, making for an absolutely cozy stay.

SOUTH AMERICA

The second-largest island in Chile, Chiloé is still something of an under-the-radar destination. But Tierra Chiloé might just change that. The 24-room resort is a boutique all-inclusive retreat on a hillside overlooking the Pullao wetlands—that includes the heated infinity-edge outdoor pool, part of the Uma Spa, which also has an indoor pool, a sauna, and a steam room. Tierra Chiloé is the perfect hub for island adventures, ranging from hiking in various parks, to a boat tour, to the craft markets of Castro, to kayaking the Rilan Peninsula.

TIERRA CHILOÉ | Sector San José, Castro, Chiloé Island, 5700000 | CHILE

THE WORLD'S BEST SWIMMING POOLS

tierrachiloe.com

SOUTH AMERICA

LAGUNA CEJAR | San Pedro de Atacama, Antofagasta | CHILE

THE WORLD'S BEST SWIMMING POOLS

Though deserts are dry environments, there's always water to be found somewhere. In Chile's Atacama Desert, which is one of the driest places on Earth, there are a number of natural pools—salt pools, to be precise, thanks to the water's high rate of evaporation. Laguna Cejar is one such salt pool, where visitors can go for a swim and experience heightened buoyancy (like what you'd experience in the Dead Sea in the Middle East). Note that not all salt pools in the Atacama Desert are swimmable. The famous Ojos del Salar, for instance, is reserved for wildlife spotting and photography.

433 sanpedroatacama.com/en/tour/laguna-cejar

SOUTH AMERICA

| | **CASA SAN AGUSTIN** | Calle de la Universidad No. 36-44, Centro, Cartagena de Indias, Bolívar | COLOMBIA |

Hidden among three historic buildings in Cartagena's Centro are the remains of a 300-year-old aqueduct, which have been transformed into a sanctuary-like L-shaped pool. It's the watering hole of the Casa San Agustin, a 31-room boutique hotel known for its restaurant, Alma, which serves a seasonally changing menu of local seafood dishes. For its small size, the hotel has an impressive list of amenities, including a spa, a library that hosts afternoon tea, and, perhaps most unique for a city hotel, a private beach on Isla Barú, a peninsula about an hour away.

SOUTH AMERICA

PIKAIA LODGE | Km 13 via El Camote, 100 meters from Cerro Mesa, Santa Cruz, Galápagos | ECUADOR

THE WORLD'S BEST SWIMMING POOLS

Given that only four of the Galápagos's 127 islands, islets, and rocks are inhabited, it should come as little surprise that most visitors to the archipelago travel by boat—more specifically, small cruises. But there are hotels to be found here, primarily on the main island of Santa Cruz. That's where you'll find Pikaia Lodge, a 14-room luxury hotel built on an extinct volcano some 40 minutes outside of Puerto Ayora. From this vantage point, the serene infinity pool has some pretty incredible views—so long as the clouds don't roll in and obscure them.

439

pikaialodge.com

SOUTH AMERICA

| | **FINCH BAY GALAPAGOS HOTEL** | Barrio Punta Estrada, Puerto Ayora, Galápagos, 200350 | ECUADOR |

THE WORLD'S BEST SWIMMING POOLS

Of the few hotels on the Galápagos's main island of Santa Cruz, none are on the beach—save for Finch Bay. It's located in the Punta Estrada neighborhood of Puerto Ayora, which is accessible only by water taxi (it's a brief five-minute ride) and has no cars. The first thing you're greeted by at the 27-room property is the pool, which separates the hotel from the beach. During the warm, dry season, it's definitely a hot spot where people congregate to cool down. Finch Bay isn't just a hotel, though—it's also a tour operator, taking guests on day trips to neighboring islands on its private yacht.

finchbayhotel.com

SOUTH AMERICA

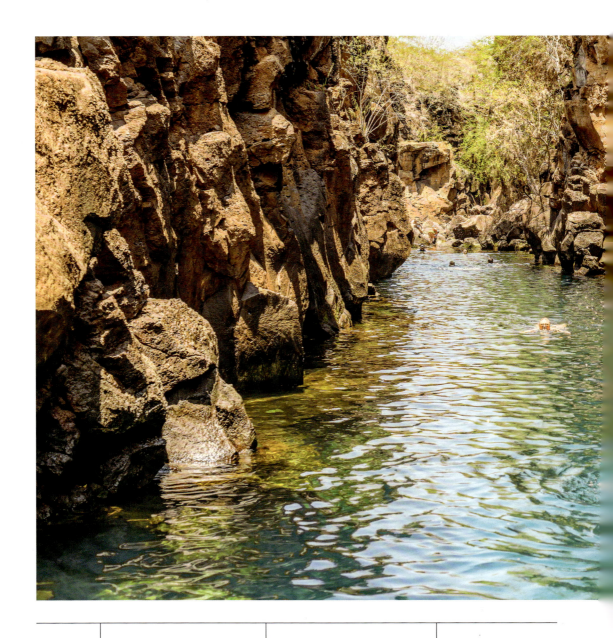

 | **LAS GRIETAS** | Puerto Ayora, Santa Cruz, Galápagos | ECUADOR

THE WORLD'S BEST SWIMMING POOLS

Just outside of the town of Puerto Ayora in the Galápagos is one of the best swimming spots on the island of Santa Cruz: Las Grietas. Meaning "the cracks" in Spanish, Las Grietas is a natural swimming hole—or, rather, a swimming crevasse. Rich blue water fills a chasm within volcanic rock, creating what looks like a lap pool with a dramatic backdrop. The water here is a combination of fresh water from an underground river on one end and salt water that comes from the sea. Before or after your swim, take a hike to the top of the rock walls to appreciate Las Grietas from above!

Credits

p. 18	© andBeyond.com
p. 22	© Oberoi Hotels & Resorts
p. 26	© Kasbah Beldi
p. 28	© andBeyond.com
p. 42	© John Athimaritis
p. 45	© andBeyond.com
p. 52	© jono0001 (iStock)
p. 54	© andBeyond.com
p. 56	© andBeyond.com
p. 58	© andBeyond.com
p. 60	© andBeyond.com
p. 66	© Rob Besant
p. 68	© Aris Vrakas
p. 74	© Tongabezi Lodge by Green Safaris
p. 78	© Amalinda Safari Collection & © Rachel Rebibo
p. 80	© Singita Pamushana Lodge
p. 84	© Frederic Lagrange
p. 90	© Ananda in the Himalayas
p. 92	© The Oberoi Hotels & Resorts
p. 100	© Courtesy COMO Shambhala Estate
p. 108	© FredFroese (iStock)
p. 109	© FredFroese (iStock)
p. 118	© The Chedi Muscat – a GHM Hotel
p. 124	© Marina Bay Sands
p. 130	© 137 Pillars Suites and Residences Bangkok
p. 132	© Four Seasons Tented Camp Golden Triangle
p. 134	© Kiattipong Panchee
p. 136	© Four Seasons Resort Chiang Mai
p. 138	© Four Seasons Resort Koh Samui
p. 160	© Four Seasons Resort the Nam Hai, Hoi An
p. 166	© Agata Kadar (stock.adobe.com)
p. 172	© Royal Champagne Hotel & Spa
p. 178	© Benoit Linero
p. 180	© Shangri-La Paris
p. 182	© Krisztian Juhasz (iStock)
p. 186	© Tropical Islands
p. 192	© Katikies
p. 194	© Katikies
p. 198	© thecriss (stock.adobe.com)
p. 204	© Cretan Malia Park
p. 206	© Cretan Malia Park
p. 218	© Luiza_st (iStock)
p. 220	© Red Carnation Hotels
p. 224	© Manuel Kottersteger
p. 226	© Angie Silverspoon
p. 227	© Patricia Parinejad
p. 232	© Damien VERRIER (iStock)
p. 238	© VOJTa Herout (stock.adobe.com)
p. 242	© Krysztof Nahlik
p. 246	© Francisco Nogueira
p. 254	© 35007 (iStock)
p. 255	© pawel.gaul (iStock)
p. 256	© Mercedes Rancano Otero (iStock)

p. 262	© jon chica parada (iStock)
p. 263	© justinessy (iStock)
p. 264	© Elenasfotos (iStock)
p. 268	© Robert Miller
p. 272	© Andy Sage (iStock)
p. 273	© Andy Sage (iStock)
p. 276	© MarcioSuster (iStock)
p. 277	© MattStansfield (iStock)
p. 278	© EcoWorld Ballymore
p. 280	© Ecoworld Ballymore
p. 282	© Thomas Faull (iStock)
p. 284	© FedevPhoto (iStock)
p. 290	© Ultima_Gaina (iStock)
p. 292	© cdwheatley (iStock)
p. 293	© cdwheatley (iStock)
p. 296	© Nayara Tented Camp
p. 300	© Jhony (iStock)
p. 320	© Douglas Ferreira (iStock)
p. 322	© javarman3 (iStock)
p. 323	© frankazoid (iStock)
p. 338	© Sheraton Waikiki
p. 348	© Kodiak Greenwood
p. 350	© Enchantment Resort
p. 352	© lightphoto (iStock)
p. 356	© RoschetzkyIstockPhoto (iStock)
p. 358	© Four Seasons Hualalai
p. 360	© CampPhoto (iStock)
p. 364	© Castle Hot Springs
p. 368	© Mirada Project – Metro Development Group – Crystal Lagoons
p. 370	© 6381380 (iStock)
p. 372	© Tanveer Badal
p. 373	© Tanveer Badal
p. 374	© Viking
p. 376	© jamenpercy (iStock)
p. 378	© ai_yoshi (iStock)
p. 382	© lovleah (iStock)
p. 386	© Matt Lauder Gallery (iStock)
p. 388	© Photo provided courtesy of the Red Moon Group Inc. Photo by Hélène Havard.
p. 390	© Four Seasons Resort Bora Bora
p. 396	© Delpixart (iStock)
p. 398	© Richard Brimmer
p. 400	© wallix (iStock)
p. 404	© samvaltenbergs (iStock)
p. 405	© mvaligursky (iStock)
p. 406	© Martin Valigursky (stock.adobe.com)
p. 410	© Four Seasons Buenos Aires
p. 412	© andresr (iStock)
p. 432	© Martinelli73 (iStock)
p. 434	© Mikaela Higgins
p. 435	© Casa San Agustin
p. 436	© Casa San Agustin
p. 440	© Finch Bay Galapagos Hotel
p. 442	© MarcPo (iStock)

TEXT
Stefanie Waldek

IMAGE EDITING
Jonathon Norcross

BOOK DESIGN
Han van de Ven

EDITING
Amy Haagsma

Sign up for our newsletter with news about new and forthcoming publications on art, interior design, food & travel, photography and fashion as well as exclusive offers and events. If you have any questions or comments about the material in this book, please do not hesitate to contact our editorial team: art@lannoo.com

© Lannoo Publishers, Belgium, 2024
D/2024/45/189 - NUR 450/500
ISBN: 978 94 014 9895 1

www.lannoo.com

All rights reserved. No part of this publication may be reproduced or transmitted in any form or by any means, electronic or mechanical, including photography, recording or any other information storage and retrieval system, without prior permission in writing from the publisher.

Every effort has been made to trace copyright holders. If however you feel that you have inadvertently been overlooked, please contact the publishers.